How to Live After 50

How to Live After 50
© Noh Jonghan

English translation edition © 2024 METASEQUO

Original Korean edition © 2023 METASEQUO
(Korean title: 오십부터는 감정을 다스려야 산다)

Japanese edition © 2023 METASEQUO
(Japanese title: 50歳からの感情コントロール)

Design © 2024 Paperzam

This book was carefully edited by a human editor
with the help of several AIs, from translation to proofreading.
The AIs used to translate and proofread this book are as follows.
Translation: DeepL, Google translator, Naver Papago
Proofreading: Grammarly

ISBN 9791193431061 (Ebook)
9791193431078 (Paperback)
9791193431085 (Hardcover)

When the days left are fewer
than the days lived

How to Live After 50

Written by
Noh Jonghan

METASEQUO

When the days left are fewer than the days lived

I was 49 years old, one year away from turning 50. Suddenly, I realized that I had reached an age where I wouldn't be surprised if I died 10 or 20 years from now. If you die in your 60s, you'll hear, "You died early in this day and age," but no one will lament that the unthinkable has happened. If you die in your 70s, you're even less likely to hear, "You died early in this day and age." Even in an era where the average life expectancy is around 80 years old, it's not uncommon to see people dying in their 60s and 70s.

I've been alive for 50 years, but is it true that I've only got 10 or 20 years to live? I don't know why I suddenly realized that, but I cannot forget my feelings at that time. It was a bit of a shock. Think about it. The 50-year was a moment, but ten years? 20 years?

When I think about it, I feel like I've been living my life underestimating my age. There was a time when books for middle-aged people dominated the bestseller lists, "Sun Tzu's Art of War for the 40s" and "The 40s, Time to Read the Analects," etc. Even then, it never occurred to me that those were the books I should be reading. I thought, "Oh, middle age is hard, and that's why these books are bestsellers." Then, I suddenly realized that I was forty and felt a little smug. Because, well, that means I'm living young.

Ten years later, now people talk about the age of 50 here and there. It feels different than when I was 40. Because I realized that the days left were fewer than the days I lived. I have just the next ten years? 20 years? I know from my own experience how short that time is. That might be why. My heart becomes anxious.

On the edge of yesterday and tomorrow

I don't know if it's 20 or 30 years or a little more, but surely the last time come. But I don't know how to live with my time left, so I'm at a loss now. It might be natural. It is because I've never really thought seriously about how to live. Isn't it everyone's life? Isn't that the way it is for everybody, to live life as it comes or as told to live it?

But when I am faced with the stark reality of my mortality, which could be "any minute now," it seems like I shouldn't live the way I've been living. I realized that if I'd lived the way I'd been living, from now on, I might as well spend the rest of my time living the way I want to live, the way I think and plan to live.

I've spent much time trying to study hard because I'm supposed to study hard, work hard because I'm supposed to work hard, and be a good husband and father because I'm supposed to be a good husband and father. While that's not necessarily a complaint, it's not necessarily an injustice, but shouldn't the rest of my time be spent on me? I don't have much left, do I?

The moment I had this apparent thought was the moment I realized for the first time in my life that I, no one else, am in charge of my life. And first of all, it seemed like there had to be an event separating the life before from the life after.

I left home with my bike, which I usually only ride to go to the local supermarket. I started pedaling from Jeongseojin. It's a slow, slow path. I went down the Han River bike path. I passed Yangpyeong, Icheonbo, Suanbo, and over Ihwaryeong Hill. I entered the Nakdong River bike path and stopped by Andong Dam. I traveled down the long Nakdong River and arrived at Daegu and Busan. I went slowly for 770 kilometers to the estuary bank of the Nakdong River. It was a journey spent entirely alone for seven whole days. It was also the first time in my life that I spent such a long time alone. The riding completely ruined my body, but my head became clearer.

From 50 onwards, people have to control their emotions

As expected, it was good to have an event. It was an event that would determine the difference between my life before and after. While I was cycling alone across the country for seven days, and even after completing the ride, I spent some time making charts, writing down lists, and imagining how I could spend the remaining time until the moment death came to me. I've been thinking about it for a year. This musing was also my first time in my life. For the first time in my life, I started living as I planned.

I mapped out my life for the next 30 years and laid out what I wanted to accomplish in 10-year increments. Along the way, I realized that no matter how many goals I set, there was one thing I needed to work on before I could achieve them: getting my "emotions" under control. To be more precise, it's about being a person who doesn't get swayed by emotions, especially when the environment around me is pressuring me in one way or another.

I'm not an emotional person. I've always thought of myself as a rational and reasonable person. But the longer I thought about it, the more I realized that being rational and reasonable might be the problem. I've come to realize in hindsight that the world, especially human relationships, is never rational or driven by reason.

In reality, being right or wrong doesn't matter as much as we think it does. It doesn't matter how much I argue with clear evidence that I'm right unless I can reach the other person's heart. Even if I'm wrong, if I can get the other person's heart, I'll gladly be accepted by them. That's the gist of it.

Yes, It's so. It is the reality that emotions rule the world, and I've been ignorant of this reality and have been arguing about right and wrong. If there were many bumps in the road of my life, those have been due to this.

I knew then that I had to confront the issue of 'emotions' seriously before it was too late. Because even if I had spent the last fifty years being driven by them, willingly or unwillingly, I would have to transcend them in the next thirty years to live the life I planned for myself. Therefore, the stories in this book reflect on how to deal with emotions in life or, more precisely, how to become an emotionless person.

From 50 onwards, people have to redesign their outlook on life

Emotions fluctuate from time to time, so it's essential to have some personalized first aid prescription. For me, there are a few prescriptions that I use as a go-to whenever I'm in a crisis. They are: eat well, sleep well, walk well, and rest well. But while these are extraordinary first-aid measures, they're not a cure-all. Sooner or later, my emotions will fluctuate again, and I'll need to sleep, eat, run, or walk again. I can't spend the rest of my life sleeping, eating, running, and walking.

So what can I do? It's pretty simple. It is what I am going to be that person. If you want to be rich, be a good money maker; if you want to be a good conversationalist, be a good conversationalist; if you want to be good at managing emotions, be a good manager of emotions. To do that, you need to take the long view and build a set of principles that will guide you through life rather than a set of first aid tips. That's why this book focuses on how to live my life and what kind of person I'll be rather than on a few emotional controls.

It takes time to become a person who is in control of emotions, a person who is not swayed by emotions. That's because as long as my life goes on, my emotions will always follow me and reveal myself. My emotions are me, so dealing with them is dealing with me. Today, I harden myself even more; in doing so, I harden my emotions even more. This process will continue in the future, and this book is the beginning of it.

C O N T E N T S

Chapter 1

"If you lose to emotions, you lose to life"

Don't get angry

Start with controlling your anger

"Anybody can become angry, that is easy; but to be angry with the right person,
and to the right degree, and at the right time, and for the right purpose,
and in the right way, that is not within everybody's power, that is not easy."

Aristotle

An incident at the district office

It happened when I stopped by the district office for business. I parked my car in the underground parking garage and went to take the elevator. The elevator arrived on the first floor, and the doors opened. A disabled man in his early 70s was pushing a motorized wheelchair, struggling to turn. He's trying to get into the elevator. Inside the elevator, everyone moved to the corner to make ample space for him to enter. Outside the elevator, people who were about to board the elevator that had just arrived stopped and moved aside.

I felt my heart soften. Caring for one another spreads warmth not only to us but also to those around us. But five seconds later, the unpleasant words that poured out of his mouth instantly froze the atmosphere.

"Oh, XX, you're supposed to get in after everyone else. XX, why are you trying to get in first, XX!"

He yelled at an older woman who tried to get on the elevator in a hurry when the elevator door opened but stopped when the electric wheelchair approached. The older woman panicked and moved out of the way, and the power wheelchair roughly dashed into the elevator, and then a mixture of unintelligible words and profanity came out of its mouth.

"XX, you help me? fuck you, officer! You XX, you mouthy XX...."

The unfortunate situation continued until I got off on the 6th floor, and even more unfortunately, he got off on the 6th floor, too. It was because the cultural industry team I would visit and the social welfare team he was likely to expect to visit were on the same floor. The sixth floor was his stage for about 20 minutes until the two friendly guards politely guided him downstairs. It was amazing to see how the social workers and security guards dealing with him were all soothing and soothing. But why was he so angry?

An incident at the Health Center

This happened, too. The coronavirus, which I had managed to avoid, had crept up on me, and it was inevitable that my family would become infected. Finally, my daughter developed symptoms, so I put her in the car and drove to the health center for a PCR test. The health center faces an eight-lane road on a busy street, and the sidewalk lanes were filled with cars waiting for a PCR test. I couldn't find a parking place, so I circled the health center on a side street and returned to the 8-lane road.

"Hey, you, fuck, you're trying to be dead? fuck, fuck!"

I looked at the side mirror on the left of my car, and there was a carnival standing slightly behind my vehicle. The passenger window of the carnival was lowered, and simultaneously, a F-word broke out. He was a man in his mid-40s. Looking slim and young, he stretched out his body toward the passenger seat with his face heated red and thrust his right hand constantly into me. His anger seemed directed at me, looking at the direction of his words and gestures. Perhaps as my car exited the back road and turned right, it crossed the left lane to avoid cars parked in the right lane, startling the carnival racing into that lane.

The parade of his insults continued until I rolled down my driver's side window and waved my hand a couple of times in apology. He rolled up the passenger window and went on his way.

But he must have been muttering "fuck, fuck" for some time afterward as my ears continued to tickle. In retrospect, he must have been breaking the F-word without realizing who he was talking to because he started swearing before I rolled down the window and turned to look at him. Then, the daughter asked me from behind.

"Dad, what happened?"
"I don't know. I think he was surprised that I interrupted him."

Why are they so angry?

Yes, he might have had a bad day for some reason. Yes, he might have been surprised. But if even so, why do people feel the need to show it so roughly that they're upset?

There are two ways to get caught up in emotions: overindulging in positive emotions and getting caught up in negative emotions. The problem with both is that we lose our composure. When we lose our composure, we lose ourselves, we lose our relationships with others, and we have a harder life than those who do not.

According to Buddha's wisdom, emotional fluctuations usually arise from the desire to distinguish between good things and bad things and try to get the good and avoid the bad. Furthermore, when a phenomenon deviates too far from our expectations, our emotions begin to flare up: if it goes better than we expected, we feel positive, and if it goes worse than we anticipated, we feel negative.

We expect a score of 80 on the test, but if we get a score of 90, we will be happy, and if we get a score of 70, we will be disappointed. When we expect kindness from our spouse, we will be more glad to receive a gift from our spouse. But if there is no response from our spouse, we will feel ignored. However, in these cases, even if we are agitated for a while, this soon returns to our composure. It doesn't cause significant problems in our daily life. However, when we expect a score of 100 for everything or when we have no expectations at all, that is, when we are always self-centered or self-deprecating, our emotions are in a constant state of instability. We are easily irritated and frequently moody.

Anger, in particular, is a typical negative emotion, and it's a short and intense way of expressing that you're in a bad mood. It takes a lot of energy, so it's hard on you and the person you're angry with. That is why people who lose their temper frequently and intensely are less likely to have good relationships in everyday life.

Angry faces are ugly without exception

Angry faces are ugly. You've probably seen it. They look like crazy people. It doesn't matter if the face is handsome or ugly. Angry faces are ugly without exception. You don't like to get close to them. You don't want to look at their face. But I have also been angry if I turn my gaze to me. For some reason, taking it out on our spouse, children, and other people we care about is especially easy.

I've been angry at my child for being spoiled, my spouse for ignoring me, and so on. When I realized that "Every angry person has an ugly face," I felt humiliated and sorry for myself for showing that face to my closest people. I immediately decided that from now on, I would at least not get angry.

The self-help bible, *The 7 Habits of Highly Effective People*, introduces the concept of an emotional bank. Every relationship has an emotional bank where trust is deposited and withdrawn from time to time. When you have a positive experience in your relationship, you can deposit trust. When you have a negative experience, you withdraw the trust. Having intimate conversations, giving and receiving heartfelt gifts, and offering sincere comfort are all actions that build trust and increase the assets in the emotional bank. Conversely, being harsh, dismissive, and angry with others withdraws trust and reduces holdings in the emotional bank.

Among them, anger is decisive because it withdraws all the assets of the emotional bank that you have gradually built up over a long time at once. Once you deplete your trust assets, it's nearly impossible for you to replenish them. It takes more time and effort than you've put in so far. In most cases, it's too hard to work on a relationship and then give up halfway through.

Therefore, it's important not to lose it in the first place. To do this, you first need to be the person who doesn't get angry. If anger is such a destructive emotion, you can manage most other emotions by practicing one thing: not getting angry. It starts with saying, "From now on, I will not get angry. Hopefully, my emotional bank isn't bankrupt yet."

== KEY POINTS ==

To become someone not swayed by emotions, you must first control your most destructive emotions, anger. Start by saying to yourself, "I will not get angry from now on."

How are the Freud soldiers in me?

"Freud's soldiers"

We are all born with 100 soldiers within us who protect our ego from the wounds we receive whenever we go through life.

The infant with no power is under stress by being controlled by the caregiver. The infant wants to crawl around and touch that beautiful thing but is restrained by the caregiver because it's dangerous. Everyone, regardless of age or sex, gets hurt when they are restrained. Two soldiers are deployed to protect themselves. A boy is embarrassed and afraid of being scolded by his mother if he makes a mistake on the blanket, even though he is old enough to cover his urine. This time, five soldiers will be deployed. At school, he was embarrassed because he was ignored in front of other children by a girl in the next class whom he had a crush on. He wanted to hide in a rat hole right away. Oh, he needs ten soldiers!

It could be a drop in the bucket compared to the full-fledged social life ahead because stories that cause extreme stress, such as failure, broken hearts, unemployment, loans, marriage, parenting, etc., will occur like a panorama. Each time, we deployed soldiers to take care of our wounded selves. It would have been sufficient to deploy a small number of soldiers if you had tripped over a stone on the unpaved road, and you would have needed to deploy a much larger number of soldiers if you had experienced hardships that seemed like your life would have collapsed.

Now, knowing how many soldiers are left in us is essential. For some people, it could be 30; for others, it could be less than 10. Then, are there enough soldiers left for me now? I don't know what I'll be going through in the future, but what if there are few or no soldiers left? What can I do? If so, I will be exposed to the wave of emotions that will come, and life will fall into rapid instability.

I heard this story of Freud's Soldiers from my close psychiatrist in private. When I first heard it, I thought it was refreshing that Freud used this analogy to describe the human ego. But when I met him later and told him that the story was fascinating, unfortunately, he didn't remember it. So, it's not clear that Freud ever used the analogy of the soldiers to describe the ego.

How many soldiers are left to me now?

Everyone was struggling when I was young, but my family's situation was much worse. My parents went out to the city in search of work, and for a year, four siblings were left in a rural house. At this time, it was probably necessary to have many soldiers.

Since then, my family's situation has remained, but I feel like I have spent my adolescence safely, perhaps because I only studied. In college, it seems that soldiers were deployed everywhere in those days because I was wandering about the inconsistency of ideals and reality that the young man at the time had, my clumsy first love, and issues of enlistment in the military.

And even when it was difficult for me to get my first job for about two years after being discharged from the military, I must have needed some.

When I recalled this period, I was sure many soldiers would be left. It was a difficult environment, but I felt I had lived well. But why was it so difficult to cope with the problems encountered while getting married, having children, and raising children afterward? Incidents, big and small, continued, the relationship of trust was broken, and I was brought to the point that I was hurt by every casual word of my wife and felt sad about the children's indifferent attitude.

"It's weird. I think I still have a lot of soldiers left...."

This one question turned things around 180 degrees. Maybe I have very few soldiers left. There must be more soldiers than I thought in the past when I seemed to have had a good life. Oh, that's why I felt it was okay! This realization allowed me to look at myself objectively for the first time in my adult life.

My younger self was overprotected by the many soldiers that were placed around me, and while the shields may have protected me from hurt, they also prevented me from communicating with the outside world. The more protective I was, the more isolated I was. As a result, I realized I hadn't had the experience of expressing myself, connecting, and being empathetic to those closest to me.

"I'm not good at empathizing or being considerate of others."
"I'm irresponsible with my surroundings, thinking I'm the only one who needs to do well."

That's how I was. When I realized this, I felt the bottom of my heart rumbling momentarily, and tears immediately poured out.

I felt sorry and sorry for myself, which must have been infinitely lonely because no one recognized me, even me. And I felt sorry for my family that had me as a husband, father, son, and sibling.

Withdrawing Freud's soldiers

So what should I do now? Walking in the fields, climbing mountains, and riding alone all day every weekend, I thought about myself yesterday, today and tomorrow. I decided to do three main things.

First, I should go back to the days when the soldiers were firmly guarding, and I should hug the young me who was still crouching and shaking. I should tell myself I'm okay now; I've grown up well and can stop shaking. If I can find stability and dare to reveal even my imperfect self to the outside in that way, I can withdraw the soldiers one by one.

Second, I need to train and augment the soldiers I have withdrawn. It's like training to control emotions, view issues with a balanced perspective, and recognize them. I'll have to organize into a force strong enough to prevent any shock easily, but I'll have to operate flexibly. It's because I have to protect myself, but I have to be open outside.

Third, I must train my inner self hard. If I do so, I will have nothing to hide and be able to exist as I am. If so, it will be safe for soldiers to become unemployed.

== KEY POINTS ==

Return to your childhood, comfort yourself, who is still shaking, and train your inner self. If so, you will have nothing to hide and be able to exist as you are.

How do words become emotions?

If you listen to his words and look into his eyes,
you can see through him. How can he hide himself?

Mencius

Words amplify emotions, and words calm emotions down. Words have facial expressions, and facial expressions reveal emotions. The emotions you convey vary depending on what facial expressions you use. Therefore, choosing and using words is controlling emotions. You should refrain from harsh, extreme, and discriminatory words and make a habit of using calm, acceptable, and neutral words in order to become a person who controls emotions without being swayed by emotions.

How to freeze the mood in an instant

"I'm annoyed!"

Whether you say it to yourself or someone else, this one word can instantly freeze the atmosphere around you. Even if the person who uttered it didn't mean anything by it, the negative energy spreads quickly, regardless of their intentions. It's like a rough concentric circle spreading in all directions when a large rock is thrown on a calm lake. Or when Elsa's magic freezes the world in the animated movie Frozen.

Moreover, if the speaker of "I'm annoyed!" is in a position of power - a mom or dad at home, a teacher at school, or a boss at work - the hearts of children, students, and employees are instantly frozen. It's like a sudden blast of cold air; they might feel the chill. It becomes an urgent matter of survival for them to stop moving and check the mood of parents, teachers, and bosses. They feel restless and uncomfortable.

This effect of negative words is actual, even if the speaker is your equal or subordinate. Even if it's not a threat to your survival, it makes you feel like something is wrong. It could be that you feel spoiled, that your authority has been compromised, or that you feel obligated to do something about it.

In addition to "annoyed," there are other common words that transmit negative emotions on a mass scale; "I'm bothered," "You have a death wish?" "You are ticking me off," "Hey, you!" and "What the hell."

How to melt a frozen mood
in an instant

I heard a story on the radio one day. It was so long ago that I forgot the radio channel, the program, and the person who told the story. Maybe it wasn't even on the radio. Anyway, a famous instructor who was active as a life mentor at the time said three words saying, "These are magic words that repair any relationship immediately," and they are these.

"I'm sorry, Thank you, I love you."

It made sense. "I'm sorry" means putting the blame on me, "Thank you" means recognizing the other person's good intentions, and "I love you" means that I'm on your side in any case. How could a relationship not improve?

I put it into practice right away. The marital relationship was cold at the time. I intentionally said "sorry" and "thank you" to my wife. I didn't dare to say yet, "I love you." I didn't do it a few times, and it wasn't even a few days. After checking later with my wife, my wife wasn't even aware of my efforts. But surprisingly, the relationship improved. No, I felt so.

Oh, this is it. The real power of "I'm sorry, thank you, I love you" was in changing my mind. It wasn't about changing the other person's mind; it was about changing my mind about the other person. The fact that I decided to say, "I am sorry, thank you, I love you," means that I changed my mind.

In addition to "I'm sorry, thank you, I love you," other words that gently convey warm feelings include "I believe you," "It's okay," "Well done," and "Okay."

The right words have power

When words are used appropriately and in context, considering the other person's mood, the words can be compelling. Follow is the story of Queen Victoria of England and her husband, Prince Albert, introduced in *The 300 Wits of Living Life*.

One day, the queen and her husband were arguing about something trivial. Because his wife was the queen, Albert had to control his temper and retreated to his drawing room. After some time had passed and the queen had calmed down, she felt compelled to apologize to her husband. The queen felt sorry for her husband, who had to live under the thumb of his queenly wife. She knocked on his living room door, which was firmly closed.

"Who is it?"
"It's the queen."

The queen spoke softly, but the door didn't open. Angry again, she sharply told him to open the door.

"Who is it?"
"I am the queen of England!"

The queen spoke solemnly, expecting her majestic words to open the door. But still, the door didn't open. Puzzled, the queen realized that her husband was the only person who could disobey the Queen of England's orders.

The queen spoke softly.

"It's me, your wife."

No wonder her husband's living room door opened. In this atmosphere, the words "I'm sorry, Thank you, I love you" must have been exchanged between them.

Words are emotions and character. Caesar said, "A sentence is determined by the choice of language used in it." If you apply this to our language habits, you know that it means the words we use daily determine our primary emotional state and shape our character. It's better to avoid words that trigger negative emotions and use words that evoke warm feelings. To do this, you need to start paying attention to your speech habits.

Words have facial expressions, and facial expressions reveal emotions. The emotions you convey depend on your facial expression, so choosing and using the right words is the key to controlling your emotions.

Cooking ramen
and controlling emotions

Men commonly think according to their inclinations,
speak according to their learning and imbibed opinions,
but generally act according to custom.

Francis Bacon

Humans have been called animals of emotion. As such, emotions are complex and tricky. It's not easy to deal with your own emotions, let alone the emotions of others. Complex and unwieldy things usually have manuals we can use in an emergency.

Why not do the same with emotions? For example, it is the "emotion manual for anytime-anywhere." If your emotions start to rise in response to a specific stimulus, follow your emotion manual. Step one: Pause. Step two: Evaluate. Step three: Act. Of course, any manual is the simpler, the better. Emotion manuals are no different.

The power of
a simple, clear manual

The simpler the manual is, the better. This manual makes it easy for anyone to utilize. Ramen recipes are a good example. We boil ramen noodles and forget that we're following the manual "How to Boil Ramen Noodles" on the back of the bag. That's how simple it is. Step 1: Bring 500ml of water to a boil in a saucepan. Step 2: Add the ramen noodles and soup. Step 3: Boil for another 4 minutes and ladle into bowls. That's the end. It is why ramen was able to become a national favorite food.

After 20 years of drinking soju with pork belly, I switched to makgeolli about 10 years ago, like a change of heart. I couldn't drink soju anymore after reading an article by an emergency medicine doctor who described the scene in the emergency room and exposed the birth, manufacturing process, and side effects of cheap diluted soju. But I couldn't stop drinking and naturally fell into the world of makgeolli, which has various charms.

I wanted to make my makgeolli instead of buying it at the store. I enrolled in a makgeolli school and took six weeks of theory and practice classes every Thursday. The recipe and manual were surprisingly simple.

Step 1: Wash 1 kg of rice and cook it with an electric rice cooker.

Step 2: Add the cooled cooked rice, 200g of yeast, and 1,200ml of water in a bowl.

Step 3: Stir the mixture morning and night for three days and let it ferment for four days.

Step 4: Filter the rice makgeolli and enjoy

The end.

As with anything, if the instructions are simple, the execution is simple. The more uncomplicated and more straightforward the instructions, the better. Because first, it's easy for beginners to master; second, anyone can achieve the same results; and third, it's easy to adapt according to your preferences and circumstances. You can follow a basic ramen recipe and add flavors like egg and scallions. You can observe a basic rice makgeolli recipe and add tangerines, watermelon, or grapes to flavor the makgeolli according to the season and your taste.

Create a simple emotion manual

Can't anyone make a manual to control their emotions, just as anyone cooks ramen and filters out makgeolli?

Emotions are phenomena that occur in response to stimuli.

When a person gets a specific stimulus, he expresses a specific emotion. If you press the red switch, the red light turns on, and if you press the yellow switch, the yellow light turns on. It's because each has a different temperament and experience. However, the manual should be simple and straightforward. Individual differences, whether red or yellow, should be aside and focus on the emotion itself for now. If so, you can respond according to the following three-step emotion manual when an emotion occurs in response to a stimulus.

Step 1 Pause:

When emotions arise, you should pause instead of responding immediately. You are buying time until you come up with the proper countermeasures. But how can you stop even momentarily when your anger starts to boil?

Leave the space physically and consciously. Take a walk, listen to music, read a book, or write with earphones in your ears. You can recite the national anthem, memorize multiplication tables, or take a deep abdominal breath.

The implementation method is different, but the key is to stay away from the stimulus that caused the emotion as soon as possible, spatially and psychologically.

Step 2 Evaluate:

There are three main things to do in the world. First, there are things you can control directly; second, things you can indirectly influence; and third, things you can't control, such as natural phenomena. Once you've calmed yourself down in Step 1, Step 2 is to assess which of these three is the specific event that triggered your emotion.

Step 3 Action:

You take action to resolve what is within your power. You can solve most of these by changing your thoughts, attitudes, or empowerment. With determination and persistence, most things are doable.

Things you can indirectly influence are usually related to other people. You can't change them directly, but you can change them indirectly by changing your thoughts, attitudes, and behavior toward them. Also, you can change them by increasing your influence. So, they may or may not change despite your will and persistence.

Finally, accept and embrace what is beyond your power. There is no point in complaining about natural disasters. It's a common phenomenon not only in nature but also in the human world. For example, it is the death of a loved one. That's why you need to learn the art of mourning.

Step 1 is a standard psychological prescription, while steps 2 and 3 are adaptations of the "circle of influence" described by Stephen Covey in his book *The 7 Habits of Highly Effective People*.

Use an emotion manual and personalize it

The simpler and clearer your emotion manual is, the better. That way, it's easy to use, and you can utilize it often enough to make it second nature. Sep 1 Pause, Step 2 Evaluate, Step 3 Act. Simple and clear as can be. Now, consciously use it until it becomes second nature. No matter how simple a ramen recipe is, it doesn't matter if you don't make it yourself. Sometimes, I'm surprised to see older celebrities on TV who can't even cook ramen, and it's because they haven't cooked in their entire lives.

If you consciously use the manual, you'll get better at it. Once you're comfortable with it, you can adapt it to your situation. It is especially true for things like the action plan for Step 1 Pause. You can choose the right one depending on your situation, preferences, and temperament. When I'm feeling overwhelmed, I walk. I walk in the mountains, fields, parks, and markets for as long as I can manage. Sometimes an hour, sometimes ten hours. Stalin is said to have been lost in thought, making shoes at the Kremlin whenever something happened to him.

The same goes for Step 2, Evaluate, and Step 3, Act. Once you become familiar with them, they become automated and personalized. Here, "become familiar" means "get to know yourself well." It is because you need to know yourself well to recognize what you can do directly, what you can do indirectly, and what you can't do. So, as you repeat steps 2 and 3, your influence grows, and your actions become more apparent.

== **KEY POINTS** ==

When your emotions start to rise in response to a specific stimulus, follow your emotion manual. Step 1 Pause, Step 2 Evaluate, Step 3 Act. Use it consciously from time to time to familiarize yourself with it.

What happens when you lock your wife in the bathroom

Do not presume that others will deceive you,
nor do you conjecture that others will not believe you.

Confucius

Our sensory abilities are worse than we think. It's impossible to perceive an object fully, and we often forget this fact. Of course, this gives us the courage to try new things. But when emotions are involved, the problem grows because we tend to look for reasons for our feelings, assume that our hunches are correct based on one or two things, and hold the other person responsible.

However, we try to ignore the fact that our brain creates our feelings; therefore, we are solely responsible for them. The other person forced to take responsibility for someone else's feelings is resentful. What happens when this happens again and again? We get stuck in a cycle of blame, anger, and resentment filling our lives, and our relationship falls apart.

The solution is to say, "I don't know," and avoid making assumptions about the other person's situation and mind. This is especially true when it comes to emotions.

The monkey who ate the pepper vs. the husband who locked his wife in the bathroom

In Hyo-rim Lee's book *Paradox Chinese Fables*, there is a story about a monkey who gets himself into trouble by unquestioningly trusting in his inadequate knowledge. This story is *The Monkey Who Ate Pepper* by Chinese fable writer Wu Guangsayo.

A monkey was traveling along a trail when he came across a tomato. It was red and plump and looked appetizing. The monkey picked it up and ate it, and it tasted delicious. The monkey had never seen a tomato before and didn't know its name, but its flavor made a lasting impression.

One day, the monkey was walking along the trail when he saw something bright red lying on the ground again. It was a pepper. It was also new to him, but because it was so red, he thought it must be much tastier than anything he had ever tasted. But instead of being delicious, it was hot. The "fire" that the monkey swallowed burned his face, his stomach, and his ass. To this day, the monkey's face and buttocks are said to be bright red.

This time, we're talking about the husband who locked his wife in the bathroom. It's from the book *Your Mind: An Owner's Manual for a Better Life* by American psychologists and psychotherapists Chris Cortman and Harold Shinitzky.

The husband was an American football fanatic. One day, he was sitting in his living room watching a football game on TV, and his favorite team was down by one touchdown in the third quarter. At that time, his wife went into the bathroom, and his favorite team scored two touchdowns to come back. The husband believed her entering the bathroom caused the team to come from behind and win, so he locked her in the bathroom until the end of the game!

Do not conjecture

While the monkey who ate the pepper and the husband who locked his wife in the bathroom seem to be competing to see who is the more clueless, we can't blame them. We're all guilty of the same thing, albeit in different ways.

If your kids don't greet you properly when you come home from work, you feel they have ignored you. But is your child ignoring you and not saying hello on purpose? They may be engrossed in an exciting webtoon or deep in thought. Despite this, it is a stretch to conclude that they're ignoring you.

When you say hello to your team leader at work, and they don't answer you but glance at you and walk past you, you feel like they are angry with you. But is the team leader angry with you? Maybe they are in a hurry because they are late for a meeting, or maybe in a hurry because they received an emergency call from the boss. It's unfair to assume they are angry without understanding these situations.

Stephen Covey, author of *The 7 Habits of Highly Effective People*, tells an anecdote. A father and his two young sons are on the New York subway. The father sits mesmerized in his seat while the boys run around the car noisily. Suddenly, the quiet subway car is in an uproar. While everyone was frowning, Kobi, convinced that the father was not doing an excellent job with his children, spoke up. He asked his father what he should do with them. The father said in a weak voice that he had just sent their mother to heaven and was on his way back. Stephen Covey felt a deep sense of shame, and only then could he see the situation in a more forgiving light.

When we stop making assumptions, we can understand and accept many things. There aren't many things in our lives that we cannot understand when we try to. To do this, we must give up the conceit that we can know everything once and for all and resolve not to make assumptions about the current situation and the other person's mind based on limited information. When we don't assume cause and effect, when we don't make assumptions, we can accept things as they are. Focusing on the present, not the past or the future, can surprisingly relax our minds.

== KEY POINTS ==

When you don't assume cause and effect, when you don't make assumptions, you can accept things as they are. Focus on the present, not the past or future, and you'll be surprised at how relaxed you feel.

How not to break down
the emotion levee
that has been built for 50 years

He that would be superior to external influences must first
become superior to his own passions.

Samuel Johnson

A dyke one thousand feet high may crumble through borings by ants

"A dyke one thousand feet high may crumble through borings by ants; a large house with a hundred feet begins with a chimney crack and burns (千丈之堤以螻蟻之穴潰 百尺之室以突隙之烟焚)."

This quote comes from Han Fei Tzu's *Euro* chapter in his book *Han Fei Tzu*, which compiled the thoughts of Legalism during the Chinese Warring States Period. Han Fei Tzu admired Lao Tzu, and the episode "Euro (喻老)" is a metaphorical translation of Lao Tzu's words.

The meaning of this quote is straightforward. Big disasters

start with small flaws, so you should always care for the little things. Baek-gyu, who controlled the river well, blocked the hole as he saw it every time he patrolled the bank, so there was no flood when he was there. In addition, older people in the family occasionally applied soil to the cracks in the chimney, so as long as older people were present, the house did not catch fire.

A stitch in time saves nine. That is why you need to pay attention to routine maintenance. If you neglect maintenance, a pea-sized ant hole can quickly collapse the bank, and sparks can fly from the incontinent chimney and burn the tiled house.

It's the same with emotions. Imagine that you have a levee inside of you that holds your emotions. Over the past 50 years, it's done a great job keeping them in so they don't overflow or dry up whenever something happens. Sometimes, your emotions explode and put much pressure on the levee; sometimes, your emotions dry up and leave the levee dry. Each time, for the sake of your family, your dreams, or just because you had to, you've been able to hold back your emotions or push through them, and you've managed to get by.

But just because it's been okay so far doesn't mean it will be okay in the future. Confucius said, "If you don't prepare for what's far away, you'll have to worry about what's near". Lao Tzu also stated, "Great things must begin with small things." You need to look at your emotional levee to see if it's okay as it is and if there's an ant hole or crack somewhere. You never know where it might burst if you don't maintain it.

Masters of maintenance - Roman emperors

The true maintenance masters in human history may have been the ancient Romans. Whether it was a republic or an empire, maintenance was one of the most essential responsibilities of state leaders. The Romans achieved a millennial empire in part because of their dedication to building and maintaining the infrastructure that formed the backbone of their empire. Consider one of Rome's most iconic pieces of infrastructure, the Roman road.

The total length of roads built by the Romans from the 3rd century BC to the 2nd century AD is 80,000 kilometers of main roads and 150,000 kilometers of branch roads. You should not ignore them just because they're ancient. The Romans dug down to 1-1.5 meters, filled it with stones, gravel, and soil, and paved the top with flat rhombus-shaped stones of 70 centimeters on all sides. The width was 12 meters. On each side, there was a three-meter sidewalk. The original purpose of Roman roads was to move Roman legions quickly, so they were made as flat, solid, and straight as possible. It could be called an ancient highway. This type of road stretched like a spider web across what is now Western Europe, the Middle East, and North Africa.

More surprising is that the roads built in the 3rd century BC were managed so perfectly by the Romans that even in the 3rd century AD, 500 to 600 years later, there was no grass in the cracks of roads. It is due to the Roman emperor and other leaders' hard work on maintenance. Maintenance was neglected after the Crisis of the 3rd Century when they were busy fending off foreign enemies from all sides. Still, medieval travelers' accounts show that the roads remained functional for hundreds of years. Some of them, of course, still carry people and cars today, more than 2,000 years later.

Emotion maintenance is essential, too

Why were Roman emperors so keen on maintenance? How did their infrastructure function so well for so long? The answer is surprisingly simple. When we think of Roman emperors, words like luxury, debauchery, and greed come to mind, but this is mainly due to popular culture, such as movies and comedies about despotic emperors at the end of the Roman Empire. However, until Rome was at its peak, Rome was ruled by emperors with a sound and rational mindset. The Roman elite was fascinated with the pragmatism of Stoic philosophy, and the emperors were the leaders who embodied this Roman spirit.

From Apius Claudius, the father of Rome's infrastructure, Caesar, the creator of the blueprint for the empire, Augustus, the first emperor who built the empire according to Caesar's blueprint, to Tiberius and Hadrian, who laid the foundation of the empire, the leaders of the Roman Republic and early empire carried out the duties of the emperor with remarkable integrity. The emperor's job was, first, to ensure the empire's security, second, to build its infrastructure. Their sense of responsibility, integrity, and pragmatism is the secret to maintenance. If Han Fei Tzu, Confucius, and Lao Tzu had known the Roman emperors of this era, they would have been the first to point to them as an example of "better safe than sorry."

It is surprisingly challenging to prepare for invisible risks. At this time, responsibility, sincerity, and pragmatic thinking provide the strength to live your daily life step by step. When such a daily life becomes a solid rock, it can be supported so that the levee does not collapse from the frequently swaying emotional fluctuations. Therefore, managing and maintaining the emotional levee depends, paradoxically, on living faithfully in a given daily life.

== KEY POINTS ==

When you have a solid foundation in your daily routine, you can keep your life from collapsing from the fluctuations of your emotions. Live your daily life step by step with responsibility, sincerity, and pragmatic thinking.

Chapter 2

"Lost, you will earn; empty, you will fill"

Don't be heartbroken

You have to let out the cry that's in your throat

Without tears in the eyes,
the rainbow of the soul does not rise.

Indian Proverb

As the years go by and you grow older, there are times when your heart becomes heavy and tearful. Isn't there a time when you were embarrassed because you got suddenly choked up even when walking in the park, listening to music, or looking at pictures?

Why does the heart feel empty when the cold wind blows and the leaves fall? It may be because now you can only afford to look back on your life. Maybe you haven't been able to care for your mind because of your work and family affairs, but now you look at it, you feel sorry that you're in tatters. Or maybe you're lonely and sad. You've been working hard, but now you realize no one around you genuinely understands your heart. You're lonesome and melancholy.

These are all signs that your heart needs some warmth right now. The first aid is to let the tears flow, not to stifle them. Cry to cleanse your emotions. Recall the good and bad memories and relive them. These will stabilize your mind.

As the years go by, why choke up?

After dinner, I take *Haki* (Bichon, 3) for a walk. We stroll through the waterside shopping district or take big laps around the ecological park for about an hour and a half. At this time, I usually listen to music on the radio with wireless earphones in my ears. It's a BGM that plays in the background of my thoughts.

A few days ago, I was walking casually with my earphones in. I listened to CBS Radio's *Kim Hyun-joo's Happy Together*, and a listener requested a song. Choi Ho-seop's *As the Years Go*. The listener said she was walking in the park and suddenly felt so emotional that she burst into tears. The host said that she understood the listener's feelings. I could understand that feeling deeply. We turned up the volume and listened to *As the Years Go Together*.

(...)
As the years go by, even if you will forget
my heart to miss you

Don't forget and remember
there was infinitely precious love for us.

This time, it was a TV program. I glanced at the TV screen in the gap before dinner and couldn't help but fix my gaze on it. The story of the couple who went to rural areas was introduced on MBC's *Tonight Dinner*. The vinyl-loving couple ran a music cafe in the countryside, and the husband's story about a customer touched my heart.

"Do you have John Baez's *The River in the Pines*?"

The owner pulled out an old LP and showed it to her; the customer who saw it suddenly began to cry. What memories would she have recalled in John Baez's *The River in the Pines*? Would it be a memory of a first love or a longing for a younger version of herself that must have been beautiful in its own right? I envied her ability to be moved by a single object.

Oh, Mary was a maiden
When the birds began to sing
She was sweeter
than the blooming rose
so early in the spring
(...)

Bursting into tears,
clearing your mind

When I think about it, I can't remember the last time I cried willingly. When I was a child, I cried a lot in front of my parents. As a teenager, I sometimes cried in front of friends. Even right before I got married, I remember once or twice when I entered the room where no one was around after a drink and feeling a sudden surge of emotion and crying uncontrollably.

That I stopped crying was after I got married. Thinking about my life, it was full of work, parenting, and family. Looking back on it now, it was a time of literal hustle and bustle to get things done before me, and I neglected my emotions. Without attention, emotions were suppressed or dulled; without them, I was no longer me.

As the years passed, those suppressed and dulled emotions, for some reason, came back to life. A single vinyl record brings back memories, a single leaf on a walkway plays an old song, and the emotions that have been revived and poured out explode into longing, bitterness, sadness, emptiness, and loneliness. I sob and burst into tears.

Everyone has a secret or two that they can't fully tell. Only I know my heart; only I can empathize with it. Existential loneliness is human destiny. You can't make anyone understand what's going on in your heart. You have to bear it alone. To do this, having an attic where you can hide anytime you want to hide is a good idea. The attic is a space where you can calmly and sufficiently mourn yourself.

It doesn't have to be an enclosed space. It could be a secluded park where you can put on your earphones and walk quietly while listening to music. It could be a nearby mountain you can hike in light clothing. It could be a corner table at a cafe with quiet music and dimmed lighting during off-peak hours. For me, the attic is my car. I feel like hiding in the attic whenever I get in my car. Then, I feel like my car hugs me warmly.

Crying has the function of purifying emotions. It makes you feel cathartic. It gives you a sense of liberation. Those who have not cried recently may be blocked somewhere in your mind. If you have a blockage, you need to break it. You need to crawl into the attic and release the tears that are clogging up the depths of your throat. Only then can you breathe; only then can you live.

== KEY POINTS ==

It's helpful to let the tears flow, not hold them back. Cry to cleanse your emotions. Recall the good and bad memories and relive them. These will stabilize your mind.

The power of conversations that don't try to win

A good word to another is warmer than linen and silk,
and a wounding word to another is deeper than a spear.

Sun Tzu

Most of the time, when a conversation goes sideways, it's because we're trying to win. What does it mean to win? It's claiming that what you say is true and what they say is false. You make it clear that you're right and they're wrong. The other person evaluated as mistaken and ignored for wrong is bound to be offended.

On the other hand, if you don't show that you're trying to win - if you don't force them to accept your facts - they don't have to be nervous. When not anxious, we're less likely to let our emotions get in the way. When we're relaxed, we can better start to exchange and evaluate facts.

Facts can't beat emotions. Even if you're right and have the facts, if your opponent's emotions run high, it's impossible to win them over with words. No amount of logic and reasoning will convince someone angry as hell. They'll get more emotional instead of acknowledging what you're saying. It's like adding fuel to the fire. We see it all the time.

If facts don't win over emotions, you should not try to win in all conversations in all your relationships. The ways to have a conversation like this are about letting go of assertiveness, not misunderstanding what the other person is saying, and being willing to support their desires.

Don't be assertive

We tend to admire assertive people. Isn't it cool to see Steve Jobs and Elon Musk? However, psychological research suggests the opposite. Japanese psychologist Yoshihito Naito describes an experiment in his book *Take Your Mind Off*.

Harold Schroeder of Kent State University in the United States had 40 men and women read scenarios about assertive men and women. The researchers expected that, based on social reputation, people would like assertive men for being manly and dislike assertive women for being unfeminine. But the results differed: The experimenters found that people view assertive men and women unfavorably.

Think of deciding what to have for lunch at work or choosing a destination for a long-awaited vacation at home. If someone asserts strongly, doesn't the atmosphere become rigid? The world usually works well, even if I don't have to be assertive to make an impact. The lunch menu is set, and the destination is decided.

Why do you have to eat Chinese food? You might eat Seolle-ongtang. Why do you have to go to Gyeongju? You might go to Yeosu. You might find a new delicious restaurant and feel Yeosu anew if you're not picky. So let go of your ego a little, and don't be choosy.

Don't be misunderstood

"You haven't done it yet?"

Depending on how you hear it, it can be an urgent reminder to hurry up or a criticism of what you've done so far, which can be off-putting. However, if it's simply a check on your current status, you can answer "yes or no" without being offended. Therefore, if the other person's intention is unclear, there is no need to prejudge and misinterpret the words as pushy or hurtful.

To avoid misinterpreting what the other person is saying, you can use the "one-third rule" proposed by communication expert and author of Relationship Conversations, Choi Chan-hoon.

When someone says something you don't like, listen to it as if they meant it with one-third the intensity you feel. For example, you could feel like, "What, are you arguing with me?" when someone says, "Have you finished yet?" At this time, you can feel like this; "I'm curious to know how far along you are." That will surprisingly ease your mood.

The one-third rule works not only when you're listening but also when you're speaking. Because the other person is listening to you at three times the intensity, you need to talk at one-third the intensity. Instead of saying, "Are you done yet?" you might say, "Can you tell me how far along you are?"

As you can see, when you need to say something negative to someone, listening and speaking in the one-third can help reduce miscommunication.

Be supportive

There are two types of people: those with a subtractive mindset and those with an additive mindset. People with a subtractive mindset see everything as a zero-sum game. For me to win, my opponent must lose. Because if the opponent wins, I lose. On the other hand, people with an additive mindset believe that the world is abundant enough for everyone to share. There is no reason to think that I have to win.

The same goes for relationships and conversations. There's no reason to insist you're right or the other person is wrong. I have no reason to win, so I can put my opinion aside and listen to and affirm the other person's opinion. Letting them decide what to have for lunch won't ruin the planet. Letting them choose where to travel won't ruin the country. Agreeing with them and letting them win won't ruin your life. It's okay to cheer for your opponent.

People feel accepted when their opinions are accepted. When you are willing to support your opponent's opinion, you can enrich the opponent's heart, and they will support you. It's a mutual enrichment. So there's no reason not to support the other person.

== KEY POINTS ==

It would help if you did not try to win in all conversations in all your relationships. It's about letting go of assertiveness, not misunderstanding what the other person is saying, and being willing to support them.

How to release the resentment in the mind

The weak can never forgive.
Forgiveness is an attribute of the strong.

-Mahatma Gandhi

In our lives, we accumulate experiences that we remember with various emotions, from happiness to depression. Some of them, especially when we are alone, suddenly come through the subconscious. It may be when washing dishes, walking, driving, or reading a book.

If remembering something or someone makes you feel good and brings a smile, that's excellent. It's like watching a heart-warming movie. But if you get a lump in your throat and a tightness in your chest, that event or person has hurt you. Whether it is small or big, it is trauma.

Most of the time, a trauma like that is not a big deal, and you can just sweep it under the rug and move on with your life. But if it keeps coming back, makes you feel emotional, and makes you want to take revenge, then it's a knot tying your life to the past. You should need to untie that knot. Only then can your life breathe, and you can move forward.

Mourning

Healing a wound doesn't mean getting rid of it. Just as physical wounds leave scars, emotional wounds leave scars. Whether it's a physical or emotional wound, it doesn't go away. It just becomes dull enough not to feel pain. Mourning is the process of dulling the pain, even when you think of hurt memories.

The repetition of the memory is itself an unconscious mourning process. It is because repeated experiences desensitize the senses. However, you don't know what you are mourning, so you can't mourn properly, and then the pain is not desensitized.

Therefore, as psychoanalyst Park Woo-ran defines it, the key to mourning is to "examine my state and emotions, observing where they come from and what phenomena they cause." The method and pace of this can vary from person to person. Digging into memories and re-experiencing them through psychoanalysis is also a form of mourning, and "looking at yourself while studying your inside through constantly reading books" is also a form of mourning. Therefore, writing this article now is a form of mourning for me.

The important thing is to go through each mourning process faithfully. You need to recall the memories, re-experience the senses, and notice the feelings you alienated at the time sufficiently and faithfully. Then, at some point, you only realize that the emotions of the past and the emotions of the present are not the same. You can face the emotions of the present away from the emotions of the past, and you experience catharsis. It is finally possible to separate the present from the past. Now, you can live a new life without being bound by the past.

So don't tell a child who cries because his toy is broken to stop crying. You shouldn't tell a rejected, unemployed, or heartbroken acquaintance to pick themselves up and move on. They should cry enough and be frustrated sufficiently. They need to recognize their feelings.

Forgiving

The wound came from the outside, but you can accomplish the mourning when focusing on your inner self. If you focus on the event, situation, or person that hurt you, you're still tied to the hurt. Like mourning, forgiveness is directed inward, not outward. If you forgive someone for someone else's sake, your feelings of injustice will remain forever. On the other hand, forgiving others for yourself restores your self-esteem, regardless of their presence.

Dr. Fred Ruskin, author of *Forgive for Good* and director of the Forgiveness Project at Stanford University in the U.S., said forgiveness is the calmness felt at the very moment when you perceive yourself as a hero, not a victim, in the process of gradually recovering your wounds, taking responsibility for your feelings, and overcoming trials. In this definition, "perceive yourself as a hero" is restoring your self-esteem.

Since mourning was a mental process that turned inward in the first place, it makes sense that forgiveness would turn inward. I understand that forgiveness is the process of restoring self-esteem, which is my inner strength. Nevertheless, forgiving is difficult because the object of forgiveness is the person who hurt me on the surface anyway. That is why Jeon Do-yeon (*Shin Ae*) suffers when she tries to forgive her son's killer in the movie *Milyang*.

According to Park Woo-ran's definition of mourning, mourning is the process of "recovering your wounds, taking responsibility for your feelings, and overcoming trials" that Dr. Ruskin discussed as a pre-stage for forgiveness. Therefore, forgiveness is a natural outcome of mourning. Once mourning is complete, forgiveness begins. If you cannot forgive, you haven't accomplished your mourning yet.

But do mourning and forgiveness have to be sequential? Remember Dr. Ruskin's declaration.

"Living well is the best revenge."

When the goal is clear, the process becomes to be simple. If your goal is to live well, you can focus on yourself, not those who have hurt you; then, you can forgive the opponent regardless of their condition because forgiveness became part of your "living well" project.

Untying the knots

In ancient Greece, there was an oracle that whoever could untie the Gordian knot would become the world's master. Many heroes tried and failed. Alexander looked at the knot, struck it down with his sword, and cut it in one fell swoop. He realized that he couldn't solve it by untying it one by one, so he cut it.

There is a similar story in China. It is an anecdote that is said to be a proverbial saying, "快刀亂麻 [que-do-nan-ma]." The story goes that Gohwan, the prime minister, gave each of his sons a piece of tangled hemp thread and asked them to untangle it. While the eldest and the youngest were struggling, the second son, Goyang, drew a knife and cut the thread in one fell swoop.

People often refer to these two stories as a bold way to solve a tangled problem. It feels cool and refreshing. Perhaps we could use this to deal with old wounds in our minds.

Mourning and forgiveness are painful, energy-intensive tasks that require us to open up old wounds until they don't hurt anymore. So why not just do what Alexander and Goyang did and cut the cord with the past at once? We can either regard that event as something that never happened in our life or that person as someone that never has been in our life!

But the quick fix is usually catastrophic. Alexander may have conquered the world, but he died at 29, and his empire was split into three. Goyang later founded the Northern Empire and became the Munseonje. But history books wrote him off as a tyrant in history books.

When I think about it, our lives resemble the process of taking time to untangle the tangled threads one by one carefully. This process is complicated and slow, so we cannot cut it off with a single stroke. If we do so, our life itself may end up collapsing. After all, living life well may be to repeat mourning and forgiveness with sincerity, taking time whenever there is a wound in our body and mind.

== **KEY POINTS** ==
After all, living life well may be to repeat mourning and forgive-

ness with sincerity, taking time whenever there is a wound in our body and mind. This process is complicated and slow, so we cannot cut it off with a single stroke.

I have the initiative in my emotions

Always do what you are afraid to do.

Ralph Waldo Emerson

Proactive people are clear in every way. Their goals are clear, their plans to achieve them are clear, and they don't hesitate to take action. When plans go awry, instead of regretting and getting frustrated, they reflect and make a better plan. When they succeed, they use it as an asset to build a better future instead of becoming arrogant or complacent.

A driven person finds and realizes the meaning of their life. They don't make excuses for their circumstances, blame others, or rely on others to fulfill their desires. They don't let the reactions and emotions of others dictate their path. A proactive person decides to take action and realize their desires.

Whether it's a relationship, following your dreams, or becoming wealthy, you must decide to take the initiative to realize your desires. Otherwise, you're giving up control of your life if you rely on external forces, such as circumstances or other people. From then on, your emotions will be swayed by external circumstances and other people's behavior.

Alexander and Caesar

One of the best examples of what it means to take the initiative is war. War is a confrontation of power and power, and it's easy to assume that the size of the force determines the outcome. But if you look at the wars that have determined history, you'll see this isn't necessarily the case. Instead, the success or failure of a war is determined by which side takes the initiative.

At the battle of Issus in 333 BC, Alexander won with 30,000 men over Darius' Persian army, which was five times that size. Alexander's strategy was to use cavalry organically to encircle and destroy the Persians, and his plan was so clear that he didn't hesitate to act on it from start to finish. The initiative was naturally in Alexander's favor, as his plan worked as intended. The war resulted in the decline of the Persian Empire and the rise of Hellenistic civilization under Alexander's control across the vast Middle East.

In 52 BC, Caesar of Rome faced a coalition of 300,000 Gaulish tribesmen with only 50,000 men. His unprecedented strategy was to besiege the enemy holed up in the citadel of Alesia while simultaneously encircling himself with solid walls and trenches in front and behind him to defend against the Gauls attacking from behind. From start to finish, the battle worked according to Caesar's plan, and the victory allowed him to decide the outcome of the eight-year Gallic War. It was the moment when all of today's Europe was incorporated into the Roman Empire.

No matter your few forces, you can win an overwhelming victory once you take the initiative. It minimizes casualties to allies, resolves quickly, and leaves a clean aftermath. The initiator clearly knows what they need to do, and they don't hesitate to execute.

We see this phenomenon not only in warfare but also in politics, diplomacy, sporting events, business, and even relationships. If initiative is essential in whatever you do, shouldn't you start realizing it in your life first?

The gap between stimulus and response

People live by accumulating various experiences while responding to internal and external stimuli. In other words, the pattern, style, and tendency to accept stimuli are the person's view of life and the world. Being a proactive person means that you choose your responses to stimuli. So, to take control of your life, you must first recognize that there is a gap between stimulus and response.

There are five receptors for stimuli: the eyes, nose, mouth, ears, and skin, which are called the five senses. As soon as the nerve cells in each organ are stimulated, the relevant information is transmitted to the brain faster than light. There is no gap between them.

The brain responds "immediately" or "reacts after interpretation" after receiving a signal from the sensory organs. Among these, an immediate response is when a signal similar to that previously classified by the brain as a signal that could lead to dangerous consequences is received. If you see something that looks like a tiger, you should immediately avoid it. You don't have time to consider whether it's a tiger. Your brain has built a mechanism called the "immediate stimulus-response" for this situation. The response is the fight-or-flight. It's often referred to as the "reptilian brain," and the work of the limbic system centered on the amygdala.

People who are frequently upset are usually governed by the amygdala, and this system has been hardwired into our brains for survival since caveman days. So, it is difficult to reject it, even if we know that modern societies are considerably safer than troglodyte societies. It's almost impossible to calm a pounding heart with your head. Therefore, there's no "gap" here either. We have to put aside the task of controlling the amygdala for now.

We have to rely on the cerebral cortex, especially the frontal lobe. All sensations are gathered and processed here. It analyzes and interprets information and commands appropriate actions. It's like a command center. Remember, it doesn't "react" like the amygdala; it "analyzes, interprets, and commands." There is a gap in between. It means that you can intervene between stimulation and reaction to secure the initiative.

Many psychological theories and psychiatric practices, such as cognitive therapy and mindfulness meditation, focus on this gap. Thinking about an event or object differently and slowing down to look at it more deeply are all ways to practice stepping in and controlling our reactions appropriately instead of reacting immediately to a stimulus. When you get this right, you take control of your emotions, and by extension, you take control of your thoughts and behaviors. When you are in control of your emotions, thoughts, and behaviors, you are in control of your life.

Fill in the meaning
instead of the emotion

An Austrian psychiatrist, Viktor Frankl, noted the gap between stimulation and reaction and developed it into a logotherapy. He was taken to the Auschwitz concentration camp during World War II, imprisoned for three years, and miraculously revived.

Frankl, who suffered all kinds of inhumane hardships at the Auschwitz concentration camp and his daughter and wife dying in a gas chamber, realized that he had infinite free space inside. No matter how much the Nazis suppressed his body, they could never invade this space in his mind. It was a gap between stimulus and reaction, and when he discovered the gap, he realized that he could choose to respond with his own will. He also decided to give meaning to his life even in extreme conditions.

Viktor Frankl shaved daily with broken glass and tried to dress neatly, albeit in worn clothes. He imagined a self-image of returning home to his wife and daughter in Vienna at the war's end and lecturing his students about the meaning of life. It was a life of squalor and despair, but when he gave it meaning, it became a life to live. Based on this experience and insight, he later proposed logotherapy, saying that it is meaning that sustains life.

Proactive people can take the initiative to get things done because they know what they need to do. People who have a clear sense of the meaning of their lives can drive their lives initiatively because they have a clear sense of what they are doing. Whatever the stimulus, their response to it is self-directed, making choices and acting according to their meaning. Alexander did it, Caesar did it, Viktor Frankl did it. Indecision, hesitation, and indecision are far from their vocabulary.

To varying degrees, I wondered if I could do the same. First, I have to recognize that there is a gap between stimulus and response and practice filling it with meaning instead of an emotional response. For example, I can start by practicing taking a deep breath and giving my children an understanding look when I don't like their behavior instead of reacting immediately with anger. It is because my relationship with my children is more meaningful than my mood.

== **KEY POINTS** ==

Recognize that there is a space between stimulus and response, and practice filling that space with meaning instead of an emotional response.

Sometimes hate and sometimes be grateful

Logic will get you from A to B.
Imagination will take you everywhere.

Albert Einstein

"Hate it but love it, love it but hate it."

It's a common saying around here. Primarily, when this phrase is used between people in a long, intimate relationship, it makes me feel like they've finally come to terms with the other person and their life as it is.

A person must make a relationship to live. Some relationships, such as those between parents and children, are formed from birth regardless of their will. In contrast, others, such as lovers, couples, and colleagues, are formed to some extent by their will. Because people of different personalities encounter each other, relation-ships, whether innate or acquired, are always dissonant. How to deal with this dissonance determines the success or failure of a relationship.

How should we deal with the discord that is inevitable in rela-tionships? Realizing that relationships are a world where hateful and pretty affection and various emotions overlap in between, you have to respond separately at that time. Otherwise, if you are overwhelmed by the intense emotions you feel toward the other person at some point, the likelihood of treating the other person with that emotion increases afterward. Only that emotion fixes the relationship. The problem becomes severe, especially when the emotion is negative.

For example, if you're hurt by an insult from your partner one day, you hate everything about your partner from that moment on. They are now an object of hate. There was a warm side, a kind side, a gentle side to them, and there still is, but now you don't see them anymore. A moment of hatred has overwhelmed them all.

If this goes on long enough, the relationship is doomed. It doesn't matter who was at fault first. Maybe you're sensitive, or perhaps the other people are insensitive. But suppose you're in a relationship where it's essential to keep things running smooth-ly, like a couple, family, or coworkers. In that case, you need to find a way to repair it. An excellent way to do this is to keep your emotions separate. Hate the person for their hurtful words. But be grateful for the kindness they show you. Stay balanced without being biased toward either one's feelings.

The illusion of a happy life

We live in a world governed by cause and effect. Every effect has a cause, and certain causes produce certain effects! An apple falls to the ground instead of rising. When you kick a stationary ball, the ball accelerates and travels, slows down due to air resistance and ground friction, and finally stops. It's clear cause and effect, and Newton showed us how it works. Einstein transformed Newton's concept of causality, which we knew to be absolute, into a relative concept. However, it didn't change the fact that our world is still governed by causality, only whether it is absolute or relative.

As such, we live in a world where causality is a given, and we understand everything with cause and effect. However, in real life, this mindset leads to biases, and the biases lead to emotional fluctuations. A typical bias is "my life should be happy." We strive to be happy and expect to get rewarded for our efforts. But life often defies this expectation. We often find ourselves unhappy despite our best efforts. The same goes for relationships. For example, "I bought a gift for you, but why aren't you happy with it?" or "I'm your wife, but why did you barely buy this for my gift?"

Why does this happen? Causality doesn't work in real life.

Life is more like a microscopic world. While the macro world is governed by causality, the micro world is governed by probability. At the quantum level, we can't predict the cause of a particular outcome or the effect of a particular cause; we can only describe that it is possible with some probability. Causes and effects are in the mix. Our world is a mixture of both.

Life is a world of random interactions of many variables. It is impossible to distinguish between chance and necessity, so it resembles a microcosm in its nature and way of being. Life is a typical complex system. It's a random mix of good and bad things, and there are only a lot of just-so things in between.

So, if you try to take just what is good for you, you defy nature, and it's even impossible. Because of that, the belief that your life should be happy is an illusion and a stretch. Similarly, the assumption that the other person should always be good to you is also an illusion and a stretch. It's never natural.

Be willing to accept all emotions

Suppose our life is a complex system and resembles the environment of the quantum world. In that case, we must be willing to accept all the emotions that arise. You can't only be in relationships with people who are good for you, and you can't only do good things for you. There are people you need to see, although you don't like them. And there are things you need to do even when you don't want to.

Furthermore, the person you hate doesn't have only the wrong side. Similarly, the things you hate to do don't have only the wrong side. There are overlapping advantages and disadvantages to the person, and there are overlapping advantages and disadvantages to the job.

Maybe he is a bossy manager at work, and employees dislike him for it, but he is a loving father to his children at home. My wife might be frowning in the morning because she's not feeling well, but she might greet me with a smile in the evening. It may be painful to work overtime and stay up all night. Still, it can bring an unparalleled opportunity to your career. You've had contracts fall through, and it's been heartbreaking, but it may also lead to more significant contracts.

What if you always try to get only good things, even in this situation? You'll get caught up in the good and the bad, your emotions will fluctuate, and you'll be at the mercy of the circumstances surrounding you and the other person in your relationship.

The key to life, especially relationships, is to take things as they come: hate when you hate and be grateful when you are grateful. To do this, you need to get into the habit of not judging, of not categorizing things as "good" or "bad." The Buddha also said not to discriminate. He said the moment we discern, we will have anguish. However, we frequently try to judge everything as a good thing or a bad thing. Because of that, we are anxious about losing what we have, and we are heartbroken about why we lost it when we lost it.

If you accept everything as it is without categorizing it, you won't have to suffer from one-sided emotions. Your mind is at peace when you take people, things, and events, whether bad or good. Everything you do will go well, and every relationship you are in, even that seemed to be broken up, will be restored. "Nature" is written as "自然 [ja-yeon]" in Chinese characters. It means "just (自) being (然)." That is also the case for people who are part of nature.

== KEY POINTS ==

Hate the words of someone who has hurt you. But be grateful for the kindness they show you. Stay balanced, and don't let either emotion dominate your mind.

Chapter 3

"Life goes on no matter what happens"

Don't be nervous

How to live
without being nervous

Clinging to what is, one falls into sassataditthi(常見 [sang-gyeon],
an unchanging truth); clinging to what is not, one falls into
ucchedadithi(斷見 [dan-gyeon], an accidental phenomenon).
Therefore, a wise person should not rely on what is or what is not.

Nagarjuna

People are anxious to have it if they don't have it, and they are worried about losing it if they have it. So what can we do to live without being nervous? Remember two things. First, fill only two-thirds of the water in a cup. Second, everything in the world flows according to the laws of necessity and chance. Whatever we do, whatever happens, by remembering these two things, we can calm the ups and downs of our emotional roller coaster ride.

Fill only two-thirds of the water in a cup

Imagine a water glass filled to the brim with water. You feel nervous that it will overflow at any moment. If you had to carry it, you'd crouch down and walk slowly, taking each step carefully, keeping the cup still in your hand. Think of a small child holding a cup full of water.

Imagine that the cup is only two-thirds full. You don't have to worry about it overflowing, so there's no hesitation in your way when you lift it and drink. You feel relaxed and bold. When the water is full, there is somehow a tension in your mind, but when the cup is free, you're not even conscious of how much water is in it. There's no room for tension.

Now, think of the water cup as our mind. Our mind is a cup that holds all sorts of emotions. It's also a fragile glass. It is a person's heart to be hurt when you are treated a little disappointed and to be flattered when you are praised a little. That's why it's a glass cup. It's because you can see the inside and it's easy to break.

What if such a fragile mind is full of disappointment and flatulence? If you have such a mind, you will be disappointed and flattered in everything, and your emotions will fluctuate wildly. The person who has to deal with such your heart will also be uncomfortable, just like when handling a cup full of water.

If you have a lot of emotions in your mind, you will be less flexible. Your thoughts become rigid, and your actions shrink. Just as you fill only two-thirds of a cup with water to make room, you should also make room in your mind. Even if you are upset, you are upset by up to two-thirds; even if you are proud of something, you are proud of something by up to two-thirds. But how can that work? To know that things in the world flow according to the laws of necessity and chance helps you to empty your mind.

All things flow
by the laws of necessity and chance

Nagarjuna was a Buddhist monk who lived in India between 150 and 250 AD. Since the time of Gautama Buddha, monk-centered Theravada Buddhism has prevailed. Still, Nagarjuna criticized it and founded Mahayana Buddhist logic, making him the second Gautama Buddha and the father of Mahayana Buddhism. In China, Korea, and Japan, he is known as Yongshu.

Nagarjuna advocated for the Mādhyamika(中觀 [jung-gwan]; Middle Way). Some say the world is made up of immutable truths(常見 [sang-gyeon]; sassataditthi), while others say the world is made up of contingent phenomena(斷見 [dan-gyeon]; ucchedadithi). In response, Nagarjuna said, don't fall for the former, and don't fall for the latter. The world lies between the two. It is the Middle Way. Worldly affairs come true in harmony with these two.

It is easy to understand if you appreciate the meaning of necessity and chance. You have to study to get good grades on the test. It is the sassataditthi, a necessity. However, studying hard does not necessarily mean you will get good grades on the test. You may catch a cold on the test day and not be in good condition. It is the ucchedadithi, chance. Like this, things happen in the world due to the overlap of necessity and chance.

By understanding the Middle Way of Nagarjuna and intensely savoring the meaning of necessity and chance, we can consciously maintain a certain level of composure. In life, we encounter all sorts of things, and we will be able to calm our nervousness a bit at that time. We won't be able to take pride excessively in the good things and won't despair in the wrong things.

Desire,
but don't cling

Chinese Buddhist scholar Fei Yong said in his book *How to Live Without Anxiety* that people want to have it if they don't have it and worry about losing it if they have it.

People want to have a good home, ride a good car, get a good job, and be successful. They are impatient and anxious to have things they don't have yet. After twists and turns, they got a good house, a good car, and a good job, and they succeeded in getting a high position, but they are now worried and anxious that they might lose what they have.

Suppose it is our fate to live anxious to desire something. In that case, we must find a way to desire to our heart's content but to alleviate our anxiety even a little. At this time, it is good to remember that we fill only two-thirds of our desire as if we were filling only two-thirds of the water in a cup and that things in the world flow through the harmony of necessity and chance.

Feel free to want a lovely house, a nice car, and an excellent job. Just make sure that "to your heart's content" is about two-thirds of the water in your glass, and accept that the outcome of your efforts will be a combination of inevitability and coincidence. Then, when good things happen, you won't be excessively proud; when bad things happen, you won't despair. You'll be able to calm your nerves and accept the world as it is.

== KEY POINTS ==

Fill the cup with only two-thirds of the water. Understand that everything in the world happens through necessity and chance. By remembering these two, you can calm the roller coaster ride of emotions whenever you feel anxious.

When to strive
and when to stop

Find your aptitude and take on a variety of challenges.
But if you have not found it by 30, don't try anymore.
You don't necessarily have to find your aptitude.

Yukio Yanagisawa

Before passion becomes poison

"You fail because you give up. Failure is an asset if you don't give up until you succeed."

"Dyson failed thousands of times but never gave up and eventually succeeded. You can do it, too."

"Be passionate. Find what you want to do and do it. Find and pursue your happiness."

Many books, lecturers, seniors, parents, and teachers all push us like this. To be successful and happy, you must be passionate, never give up, and do it until you succeed. It may be true for some people, but it's usually a lie for many.

We all know from experience that there are many things that we can't do. We might often not figure out what we like, no matter how hard we try. We spend our whole lives trying to be successful and happy, and most of us don't succeed, so we're not satisfied. The heart is empty, and impatience and anxiety fill it. But is it impossible to be happy if you're not successful, and is it even necessary to be happy to live a good life?

The trend of "political correctness (PC)" has been spreading like a fashion around the world for some time. It's a social movement that rejects discriminatory language in all areas, including ethnicity, race, gender, religion, disability, occupation, and age. Everything has light and shadow, and there are advantages and disadvantages. It is the light that has contributed to eliminating discrimination and prejudice. Still, it is the shadow that has resulted in the shrinking of diversity and the amplification of conflicts by imposing a one-size-fits-all approach. A medicine is a poison if used too much, and a poison is a medicine if used in moderation.

The belief that you should succeed in life, find your aptitude, and follow your passion seems to have turned into a kind of "Correctness" at some point. It's a lovely saying and an encouragement for a better life, but when enforced in a one-size-fits-all way, it can make us feel like being left behind. As a result, we feel like we're doing something wrong if we don't try hard enough to succeed, we feel like we're doing something we're not cut out for, and we envy those who are passionate and feel pathetic that we're not. Passion is no longer supportive; before we know it, it becomes toxic.

Strive,
but don't have to strive to die

Each person only lives their own life, and it is natural that each person's life is as diverse as the number of people on Earth. It's a life that can't be measured by one or two criteria that ignore its diversity.

When you stop clinging to a single set of beliefs and let go of ingrained stereotypes, you open up a whole new world of possibilities. My life doesn't have to be successful. My life doesn't have to be happy. I may desire it, but that's never natural. Nature is nature because it is itself. So it's natural even if we fail; it's natural even if we give up. Of course, it's natural even if we're not happy.

If we accept that humans are part of nature, then success or failure is natural in itself. When we realize that there is no reason we have to be successful or happy, we can finally say that we are okay just the way we are and that others are okay just the way they are.

All living things strive to survive. Without striving, they cannot survive. Strive is the reason for existence. The leaf-rolling weevil strives to build its nest, the Formica hayashi strives to repair its anthill, and the bumblebee strives to get honey from each pumpkin blossom. We strive, too. We strive to get promoted, make sales, get along with people, and write books.

Striving is to put the will to create something into action. It's a creative act. Creating is an art, and that's why striving is beautiful in itself. It energizes our daily lives and makes us feel alive. Passion fuels this creative act. But just as too much firewood can put out a fire, too much passion can put out a creative fire. Now, we don't know why we're trying, and from then on, the more we strive, and the more we fuel our passion, the more anxious, nervous, and impatient we become.

Strive, but if you can't find any meaning in it, you should stop striving. You don't have to strive to the point of death, gnawing away at your life force. Trying too hard is never natural. When you stop striving unnaturally, the tension, anxiety, and impatience that have filled your mind will dissipate, and serenity will take its place.

== KEY POINTS ==

Strive, but stop striving if you can't find any meaning in it. You don't have to strive to the point of death, gnawing away at your life force.

Stopping
excessive power

If you are depressed, you are living in the past;
if you are anxious, you are living in the future;
if you are at peace, you are living in the present moment.

Lao Tzu

To move against water, you must use excessive power. To run against the wind, you have to use excessive power. This power is beyond your ability and that you exert to satisfy your excessive greed. When you are tired and have to gain strength again, and when you have to turn in a different direction than you have ever been, excessive power helps you for a very short time.

But that is all. You must let go of your excessive power and return to your original power. That way, you can last a long time. The rest of your life is still long, and you have a long way to go. Now, you must let go of your excessive power and go at a speed that suits your power.

Don't follow a salmon

The sight of a salmon making its way up a river is glorious and majestic. Even as they're being pushed and pulled by the rough water, they're pushing themselves forward, flapping their tails and bodies from side to side. After many frustrating attempts, they manage to jump several times higher than their body length. They don't care even if rocks or boughs scratch them in the water. Their will to climb back up the river is phenomenal and seems reckless. But why do they have to exert so excessively?

This excessive power of salmon is the last struggle of life. It's the ultimate passion to return to where it was born, lay eggs that contain new life, and end its life. Therefore, the salmon's excessive power has a tragic beauty. As glorious and beautiful as the salmon's last struggle is like this, we can't live as if today is our last. We have tomorrow to live like today.

I often had to pass by endless riverbanks when cycling around the country. In particular, the Nakdong River is wide and long, so there is a lot of wind. Strong winds blew in front of me or from behind. When the wind was against the back, the wind pushed me from behind, and I could save power and speed up the pedal. On the other hand, when I faced the wind, the wind wall blocked me, and it was hard to go forward.

To maintain my speed in a headwind, I must exert excessive power and take the result of losing energy. If I take my excessive power out at this time, I can maintain my stamina, even though my pedaling slows down and my speed drops. I have to ride my bike tomorrow, and someday, I will reach the lower bank of the Nakdong River. I cannot imitate the glorious struggle of salmon.

Make a plan,
but don't get stuck

Excessive power is a force for overdoing; it comes from a desire to carry out your intentions. You use excessive power when you try to get something done that you can't do. Therefore, to put down this excessive power, you should not be trapped by your intent. Make a plan, but avoid getting stuck in it. You should flexibly think that you can withdraw your intentions along the way; you can modify your plans along the way. If you insist on sticking to the intentions and plans in your head, you will use excessive power force when a counterwind blows.

After Shakyamuni attained enlightenment, he gave sermons to many people in many places. His teachings to sentient beings are brought together as one. It is the path to liberation. However, sentient beings have different circumstances and are at varying levels of receptivity to the teachings. Therefore, the Buddha used various analogies to describe where sentient beings are and where they need to go, such as the "burning house" and the "eastern Dharma world," depending on who is listening, when he explained how to reach liberation. That is why many versions of the Buddha's teachings exist, from *The Lotus Sutra* to *The Heart Sutra*.

After saying so much to lead sentient beings to liberation, Shakyamuni told them to forget everything he said. It's a reversal. Shakyamuni's meaning is clear. Don't get caught up in words. Even if they are the words of a Buddha, when we get stuck in words, we lose sight of the ultimate goal of liberation. It's like we see the finger pointing at the sun, although we have to see the sun. Suppose we're stuck in the Buddha's words, forgetting the end goal of liberation. In that case, the words of the Buddha also become an excessive power.

So, make a plan, but avoid getting stuck on it. Think big and wide, but make specific actions small here and now. Even if you aim for the lower bank of the Nakdong River, the final destination of cycling around the country, you should obey the causeway and the wind in front of you here and now. Even if you envision yourself living in a big house, you must adapt to a dilapidated house here and now. Even with big goals, you must take small steps here and now. You have to let go of your excessive power. Otherwise, you'll quickly run out of steam and never reach the end.

Live in the "here and now"

"If you are depressed, you are living in the past; if you are anxious, you are living in the future; if you are at peace, you are living in the present moment."

It is Lao Tzu's words. Lao Tzu advises us not to be bound by the past, not to be bound by the future, and to live in the here and now. If you do not force yourself to do so, it is possible. The past and future are the wind that blows. That's it. Don't try to stop the wind from blowing. When you let go of excessive power, your mind becomes peaceful.

== KEY POINTS ==

You must let go of your excessive power and return to your power to last a long time. The rest of your life is still long, and there is a long way to go. Now, let go of your excessive power and go at a pace that suits your power.

The homework as a life given to me

The man who is swimming against the stream
knows the strength of it.

Woodrow Wilson

I once stared for a long time at the serious face of a child doing her homework, holding her pencil short and pressing it firmly into her notebook. Suddenly, I had an "aha!" moment. It was like realizing a piece of life's truth.

"Oh, that child is living her life with integrity right now!"

Wouldn't it be the same for our lives? As we get older, we are constantly getting homework. It's useless to question why these annoying or difficult tasks were given to me as homework. It's just given. Sometimes, I can manage to take my time, and sometimes, I'm bothered or have a hard time, but I can't pass it without doing it. No one does my homework for me. No one lives my life for me.

In life, there are times when the weight of life is challenging for me. I wonder why I'm the only one with a heavy burden while everyone else lives a carefree life. At such times, I feel a little lighter when I think that the teacher of life has given me such homework. There's no need to ask, "Why me?" I was born, I have to live, and as long as I have to live, I have to do my given homework. As Schopenhauer's insights, humans only live with a "will to live."

"Kim Ji-young, born in 71" vs. "Emperor Julian, born in 331"

It is the story of an acquaintance. She was born 53 years ago as the eldest daughter of a low-income family, and her family was constantly in need. She attended a night commercial high school, working in a factory during the day and studying in the classroom at night. She married her first husband because she loved him, but he was not a man who took care of the home. He abandoned his wife and two young children.

After the divorce, she raised her two children alone, doing odd jobs. It was a tough time for her to worry about putting food on the table. On top of that, her oldest child was a troublemaker growing up and did not decrease when he grew up. Time and time again, her hard-earned savings went into repeatedly cleaning up the child's accidents. Even now that her children are grown, she spends most of her time doing hard labor and cleaning up the accidents of the older child. Fortunately, is it a small consolation that her second husband is kind?

When Julian was six years old, Constantius, who had taken over from his father as emperor, launched a massive blood purge in which Julian's father was also killed. Young Julian, along with his barely surviving half-brother Gallus, grows up in a dilapidated citadel far from the city center under the watchful eye of the emperor. The brothers can do nothing to develop into talented men except survive.

As time passed and Julian became 20 years old, his brother Gallus was chosen by Emperor Constantius to become a "junior emperor," only to be executed at the emperor's whim. Julian's fates take a sharp turn. At 24, he was ordered to succeed Gallus as "junior emperor" and rule over what is now Europe. It is from the same suspicious emperor who killed his father and brother. Will he be able to survive?

Julian, who had never been trained in politics, had never been trained in the military, and had all he could do was stay alive, took his homework seriously. And at that moment, a miracle happened. He defeated the barbarians, earned his soldiers' respect, improved his people's lives, and became emperor four years later.

From "will to live"
to "wisdom of life"

People who believe life should be exceptional cannot understand people who live and have to live hard lives. Those who believe that having and fulfilling dreams and goals is the only way to live tend to ignore them and underestimate them, saying, "Why do they live like that?" Or they are seen as objects of pity, saying, "How do they live like that?" Sure, maybe that's how they see their own lives.

However, it's a different story if we look at life as a process of silently completing homework assignments. It is because, whether homework is difficult or easy, their willingness to do it to the end is noticeable. Sometimes, I feel that determination unexpectedly when they say something like, "What should I do? I have no choice but to do it." Looking at their faces, I recall the serious face of a child doing homework with her mouth closed. And without realizing it, my mind becomes solemn. Isn't it beautiful to see someone doing what they are doing seriously?

Schopenhauer recognized that people's "will to live" is so strong that it overwhelms all other values, such as honor, power, knowledge, and success, and that this "will to live" drives each person to live their life. According to him, to live a happy life, we must recognize this "will to live" inherent in us and deal with it well, and this technology is the "wisdom of life."

So, if I am going through a difficult time, this could be an excellent opportunity to recognize the "will to live" within me and develop the "wisdom of life" to manage it better. It's not just a matter of lamenting and wondering, "Why is my life going so badly?" I will keep Schopenhauer's wisdom in mind whenever I deal with my life. If I do my homework, as Julian did, I will not only have the "will to live" but also the "wisdom of life."

From Heaven to Hell, from Hell to Life

It is the story of another acquaintance. He was once the CEO of a successful small and medium-sized company. His company was listed on the KOSDAQ, and its annual sales reached 80 billion won. It is said that haste makes waste. The company that proliferated collapsed quickly. The company promptly went bankrupt and was soon liquidated. All that was left was a pile of debt that would take a lifetime to pay off and a foreclosure notice.

For a while, he was deeply frustrated. But in the end, he decided to do some homework rather than give up everything. He decided to share his story of failure. He wrote a book about his successes, downfalls, misjudgments, and mistakes along the way. Since then, he has continued to do his homework while serving as a president consultant, helping small and medium-sized business owners start and run their businesses.

We all have our homework to do. How heavy it is is determined by fate. It is the same that I can't choose to be born into a wealthy family or a low-income family. But this doesn't mean I can sit around comparing the weight of other's homework to mine. If I am willing to accept my homework and do it, that is, if I discover and exercise the "will to live" that is latent in me, I can reach a state of mastering the "wisdom of life" that transforms my destiny into my own life.

== KEY POINTS ==

Humans have to live because they are born. And as long as they have to live, they have to do their homework given to them. As Schopenhauer discovered, humans only live with a "will to live."

When you feel empty, take a quantum jump

The greatest risk is the risk of riskless living.

Stephen Covey

There are times when we're going about our daily routine, and suddenly, our mind goes blank. Suddenly, we feel empty and wonder what the meaning of everything is. How we deal with this feeling can make all the difference in the rest of our lives.

A light drink can appease us, and we'll live as we used to. That's fine, though.

If we take it a step further and start a hobby we've always wanted to do, we'll be able to spice up our life. That's fine, too.

But if we go one step further and try something we would never do normally, our whole life may change. Miracles happen.

When life begins to change

How does life-changing change begin? When you listen to the stories of successful people, you will know it's often after a life-altering event, such as a job loss, divorce, rejection, or business failure. If you think your life has hit rock bottom, feel disillusioned with your life, and realize that you can't live like this anymore, it's time you decide to make a new life.

Jinnosuke Kokoroya worked in sales at a large company. He was a steady and responsible model employee. He was sincere enough to do not only his own work but also others' work. He worked at the expense of his whole life. Naturally, burnout set in, and to make matters worse, his wife left him. He thought he would die if he continued to live like this, so he dropped everything. In his struggle to survive, he studied psychology and found it healing. Finding solace in psychology, he studied psychological counseling, hoping to help others with the same difficulties.

Today, Jinnosuke Kokoroya is one of Japan's most famous psychotherapists. Many people from all over Japan come to Kyoto to hear him speak, and his students, who have completed his particular training program, scatter across the country to heal people's hearts. He touches people's hearts through counseling, lectures, publications, and blogs. He started walking the path of a musician, which he had dreamed of since he was young but had put off because he was busy. And now he holds psychological concerts yearly at large venues to gather his fans.

Seo Mi-sook used to be the aunt of a jjimjilbang cafeteria. She quit her private academy and got a job at a jjimjilbang cafeteria to earn a living; one day, she heard her daughter cry and tell her that she had failed her final interview to become an announcer. She was heartbroken because her child's repeated failures seemed to be due to her poor parents, and she decided that she would not live like this anymore.

At first, she started getting up at the crack of dawn. She searched and read books by successful people, studied how to make money, created blog content on the topic of "Living for a Week with 70,000 Won for Food," published it as an ebook, and gave lectures. She gradually expanded his investment area from using reward apps to stock investing and real estate investing. She put all this experience into a book, *How to Challenge and Get Rich After 50*, which became a best-selling book. Today, she is an active speaker, entrepreneur, and investor. All in just one year.

Intentionally creating inflection points for change

Whether it's Jinnosuke Kokoroya or Mi-Sook Seo, people who have succeeded in changing their lives seem to have begun to change in the wake of the crisis of desperation. However, if you look closely, you'll find that it's not the crisis itself but the realization that "I can't live like this" and the determination to "live differently from now on" that sparked the change. If so, you don't have to go through a crisis to be enlightened and make up your mind. By intentionally creating an inflection point, even the most unremarkable of us can begin to live a slightly different life.

Suppose you decide to create an inflection point intentionally. In that case, you should try something you would never do or thought you couldn't normally do. It's not the kind of thing you could do with a bit of courage, but the kind of thing you'd think is impossible. Then, you can quantum jump from this life to that life at once. Quantum jumping consists of changing your attitude and thoughts about life 180 degrees.

For example, you could buy a new car that costs two to three times more than your current car. The price is important, but it's more about whether you really desire the car. Find a car that makes you say, "Oh, this is my car," or "I'd die if I didn't have this car." Embrace that car and miss it like crazy. When a week goes by, and you can't stop thinking about it, and a month goes by, and you can't stop thinking about it, it's time to take the quantum jump. Don't go back and forth; sign the contract. Think that it'll work out. The "you" who drives a car you really desire is different from the "you" who drives a car, depending on your financial situation.

How far have you been riding your bike? If you've only been thinking about riding a bike when you're going to the local supermarket, grow that idea. Jump 10 kilometers round trip, 50 kilometers round trip, and 100 kilometers round trip out of town. Once you can ride 100 kilometers for 10 hours a day, it's time to make a quantum jump. On the spur of the moment, ride the longest bike path in Korea. It stretches from Jeongjeongjin in Incheon to the lower bank of the Nakdong River in Busan, covering more than 600 kilometers. If you stop at Andong Dam along the way, it's more than 700 kilometers. In just one week, you can make a quantum jump. The you who used to ride a bicycle to the local supermarket and the you who completed the national riding are different.

Do something you thought you couldn't do

If you think these things are impossible, you are mistaken. I've done them all. Before I did them, I thought they were impossible, too. After doing things that seemed impossible, I realized that I was no longer the person I was. I felt my self-esteem rising. I was less hesitant and tried new things with a lighter mind than before.

If you envision a new you but don't want it to remain a fantasy, you shouldn't live the way you've been. You need to change and create a trigger to change, even if it's on purpose. It's a matter of changing 50 years of hardened thoughts and temperament.

Small changes cannot make a new you. You need a big change, you need a big trigger, you need a quantum jump. To do that, you need to think and try things that you would never have done and would never have been able to do. That is the boundary that separates the "you of yesterday" from the "you of tomorrow."

You can't do something because you haven't tried it, not because you can't do it. It seems impossible because you don't think about trying it, but once you try it, it's surprisingly simple. Once you've made one or two quantum jumps, you'll have the strange experience of convincing yourself that you can do it when you wonder if you can. And at some point, the empty heart turns into an unknown excitement.

== KEY POINTS ==

How you soothe your empty heart will determine the rest of your life. If you soothe it with a light drink, you can live as you have always lived. And if you try something you would never do in a normal life, your life will change.

Chapter 4

"Thinking of the yellow-bellied goose bug at the end of the universe"

Don't be nervous

Imagine the entrance to death from the entrance to life

We forfeit three-quarters of ourselves
in order to be like other people.

Arthur Schopenhauer

No matter how big a deal it seems, it's small in the face of death. Even what seems like getting into big trouble if you don't do it now is as light as a feather compared to the weight of death. Whether it's a job you're doing, a relationship you're in, or a dream you want to fulfill, if it's causing you emotional turmoil, take a moment to imagine the death of yourself. All issues are submerged in the face of death.

What happened in "my funeral"

There's a book I always read every December. It's *The 7 Habits of Highly Effective People* by Stephen Covey. This time is my fifth year reading it. I don't just skim through it; I read it deeply, underlining meaningful sentences and taking summary notes in the margins. Of course, the book is relatively thick, but the bona fide reason it takes me a month to get through it is this habit of reading. It's a great way to end the year and start the next one fresh.

Every year I read this book, it strikes me differently. Some years, it's leadership; some years, it's relationships; some years, it's time management, and so on. The book is a good guide for me, depending on my situation. One year, I was struck by a scene describing a near-death experience. I found it reverent and beautiful.

I imagine myself leaving my physical body. I step out of my body and look at myself. I see an old, decrepit body. I see my family around me, some crying, some sobbing, some turning their heads to stare into space. I am dead.

The next scene is my funeral. There are a lot of people gathered in a very solemn atmosphere. My eldest son and daughter-in-law, my eldest granddaughter, my spouse, my coworkers, and my friends from my social circle say a few words.

"He was always so kind and generous."
"He had a strong sense of responsibility and never gave up."
"He was strong on the inside and soft on the outside."
"He always smiled and made people feel comfortable around

him."

As I listen to their words in silence, I tear up. I feel like I lived a good life; maybe this is the "I" I want to be. But what if I step out of my imagination and into reality? Am I kind, responsible, firm on the inside, soft on the outside, and smiling now? If not, why am I not living the life I want to live?

All issues are submerged in the face of death

If I think about it, the evaluation of myself that I want to hear at my funeral may be the way I want to be. And becoming that person would be the meaning of my life. And yet, I often forget that meaning and become the person I don't want to be. I am angry, irritable, reprimanding, criticizing, and impatient.

I often nag and scold my children because they don't answer my questions, stay up late to play video games even though they have a test coming up, and their beds and desks are always messy, but do they "really" deserve to be scolded?

I often criticize my spouse because she often forgets my birthday and our anniversaries, spends a lot of money, always droopy on the sofa when she gets home, puts off doing the dishes and cleaning, and does not manage her body, but does she "really" deserve to be criticized?

A coworker at work who can't seem to get things done but always talks about other people's business, retirement or termination that I'm not ready for yet, things I want to buy, things I want to do, a small income but a lot of spending, etc. These things make me feel upset, anxious, and impatient, but are they "really" something to be so obsessed with?

It's easy to lose my bearings when my emotions are running wild. When I lose my bearings, I need to pause. And then I fly to my funeral, which could be someday. Who do I want to be? Probably not the parent who nags my children, the husband who berates my spouse, or the coworker who is picky about everything. Once I find that version of myself, my attitude toward them will be different, my feelings will be different, and then their attitude toward me will be different. Even better, maybe they'll listen to me.

It's matter that who I want to be

Futurist and best-selling author Daniel Pink analyzed 16,000 people's "regrets" and wrote *The Power of Regret*. According to him, regrets can be classified into two categories: regrets for doing something, and regrets for not doing something. However, regrets for not doing something are twice as common as regrets for doing something. It means that people usually regret something, saying "I should have done" more than saying "I shouldn't have done."

It's better to regret doing something than to regret not doing it. So, what can you do to ensure you're happy with what you've done? Take a look at the four most common types of regrets people have. In the book, the four types of regrets are:

Foundational Regret for not having a solid foundation, such as healthcare or savings.

Boldness Regret for not having the courage to take on challenges.

Moral Regret for doing wrong to people close to you.

Connection Regret for not seeing and staying in touch with people close to you.

So, what I need to do is to build a solid foundation in my life, challenge myself to do what I want, and stay in touch with my loved ones. But furthermore, what can I do to avoid regretting what I did? It also comes back to the fundamental question.

"What kind of person do I want to be?"

Again, I imagine my funeral. I want people to remember that I was kind, responsible, strong on the inside and soft on the outside, and always smiling. If I use this as my guiding principle in whatever I do or whoever I meet, I'm less likely to be swayed by circumstances. If I am consistent in my feelings, thoughts, and actions, I will have fewer regrets.

== KEY POINTS ==

Whether it's a job you're doing, a relationship you're in, or a dream you want to fulfill, if it's causing you emotional turmoil, take a moment to imagine the death of yourself. All issues are submerged in the face of death.

Physical strength is emotional strength

Emotions are the brain's interpretation of the body's reactions caused by hormones. The body releases certain hormones in response to certain stimuli, which the autonomic nervous system detects and triggers specific physical reactions. It's like breaking out in a cold sweat, heart racing, or hair standing on end. Then, the brain interprets this as "excitement," "love," or "fear." When the body is refreshed, emotions are refreshed, and when the body is sick, emotions are painful.

Therefore, physical strength is emotional strength. To be more precise, physical condition determines emotions to a large extent rather than physical strength itself. You only have to look at Nick Vučić, who lost both his arms and legs, to see how joyfully he goes about his daily life with just his torso and head. When you keep your body in optimal physical condition, you keep your hormones in optimal balance. When your hormones are in optimal balance, you can minimize the ups and downs of your moods and stay calm.

What to include in your to-do list

In life, you have to meet a lot of people and deal with a lot of things. To keep your life from being controlled by others or external circumstances, you must do what is precious first. You must take care of your precious person first. You must do what is precious first. Place what is precious on the life schedule first and place the rest later.

Naturally, physical activation should be at the top of your to-do list. Your thoughts, feelings, and behaviors are all the work of your body, so keeping it in optimal condition should be your priority. And yet, most of us do the opposite. We work, study, socialize, sleep, eat, watch TV, etc., and only after we've done all that, or even after lying around with nothing to do, do we suddenly feel guilty and think we should exercise.

If you want to achieve different results, you need to act differently. If you feel like your emotional state is unstable for no apparent reason, your physical condition is likely broken. If you're not rested enough, try resting; if you're not sleeping enough, try sleeping; and if you're feeling stiff, try moving around a bit. As your body improves, you feel energized and lighthearted. Build up this experience slowly, once or twice.

It's important to consciously recognize and remember these small experiences, these sensations of change, and try to recreate them repeatedly. If you let it pass, it's just another moment in your day that passes by countless times. Still, if you remember and repeat it, it becomes a habit, and a habit can be a potent life-changing weapon.

Simple ways to create habits

Now that you've decided to put physical activation at the top of your priority list, you must stick to it. Still, it's not easy. It's because that's annoying and hard. To keep doing the things you don't want to do, the things that bother you, the hard things, you need to make them a habit. That way, you can do it without being pushed by the "trivial matters" frequently rushing in, and you can minimize procrastination because you're lazy.

A habit is a regular form of behavior, an automated pattern of action. You can get into a habit when you consistently do a certain amount of work at a certain time in a certain place. The timeframe for habit formation is often referred to as 21 days or three months. Still, these numbers are meaningless to the individual. Until it doesn't bother you, until it's something you don't have to think about, until it's something you do naturally, you're bound to fail and try again.

There are some tips to help you form habits that many books and successful people offer. One of them is to minimize the room for the troublesome mind to intervene. If you want to create a habit of jogging in the morning, reduce the amount of preparation you have to do between waking up and going outside. Leave your workout clothes by your bed, or even sleep in them and place your sneakers in the direction you head out the door. That way, you're ready in three steps: wake up, go straight to the front door, and wear your sneakers.

Another thing is to build up small successes. If you manage to run a kilometer two days a week this month, you can try to run two kilometers three days a week next month, and so on. Like "taking titles" or "leveling up in a game," the feeling of accomplishment at each step will motivate you to keep going.

It's also good to imagine the "you" who you want to be after some time. Imagine yourself losing about 2 kilograms by walking fast or running slow at 5 kilometers per hour for an hour a day for two months. There's no reason not to stick with it, even if it's annoying and hard now. The goal shouldn't be too far away, maybe a month or two or half a year, so you don't feel overwhelmed and feel like you can do it.

The power of the habit of exercising

In my experience, 30 minutes on the treadmill and 30 minutes of strength training, such as dumbbells, every day for a year are enough to lose around 5 kilograms without yo-yo-ing. As I lose weight and my core muscles hold up, I feel more balanced and, most importantly, healthier. A lighter body is a lighter mind. Other people's eyes are the first to notice and tell you about the changes. When you feel that you are fit in this physical condition, you can lower the intensity a bit. After that, you may maintain your status with an hour of walking three to four times a week and an hour of strength training two to three times a week.

The power of the habit formed in this way is more potent than expected. It's hard to reverse a habit once it's formed, and while you establish your habit, other unnecessary habits naturally disappear. While you exercise at a certain time, in a certain place, the things that get in the way of that will naturally disappear. No more going to bed late, no more drinking in the evening, no more endless hours staring at the TV. That time is filled with exercise, walking, reading, writing, and studying. Daily life becomes simple, focusing on what is essential, and the emotional state also becomes simple. It's all thanks to your exercise habits.

== KEY POINTS ==

When you keep your body in optimal physical condition, you keep your hormones in optimal balance. When your hormones are in optimal balance, you can minimize the ups and downs of your moods and stay calm.

Thinking of
the "yellow-bellied goose bug"
at the end of the universe

My sense of God is my sense of wonder
about the universe.

Albert Einstein

How far is the universe?

Imagining outer space is awe-inspiring.

We often picture the solar system with the sun at the center and a line of nine planets from Mercury to Pluto. But the reality is different. If you isolate the solar system in space and look at it from a distance, all you would see is the sun. Remember that the sun is 696,340 kilometers in diameter, the Earth is 6,371 kilometers in diameter, and the distance between them is about 150,000,000 kilometers. In between is Mercury, which is one-third the size of the Earth, and Venus, which is the size of the Earth, but it's safe to say that there's nothing between the Sun and Earth.

The situation is the same from Mars to Pluto. And the nine solar system planets aren't even lined up in a straight line. They're scattered far away (even this word cannot correctly explain the reality) from the sun, and their tiny presence is almost pitiful. So, the solar system is just the sun. It's a nearly empty space with nothing but the sun. You can ignore the Earth here.

Now consider the star known to be closest to the sun, Proxima, which is in the constellation Centaurus. At 107,280 kilometers in diameter, it's about one-seventh the size of the sun. This star, whose name is also unfamiliar, is about 4.244 light-years away from us. At the speed of light, it would take us four years and one more season to get there. Light travels 300,000 kilometers per second, and it takes about 500 seconds, or just over eight minutes, to get from the sun to Earth. Can you imagine how far away Proxima is?

Like the solar system, the Proxima system is probably empty. If you isolate the solar and Proxima systems in space and look at them from a distance, you would see nothing but two dots in a vast expanse of space. It's a literal void.

Who am I, and why am I here?

If we expand our thinking in this way, the universe is empty. The solar system is empty; the Proxima system is empty; our galaxy where they gather is empty; the giant galaxy where the galaxies gather is empty; and the universe where "empty"s gather is empty.

Don't be misled by the countless stars in the night sky. They only show how wide and deep the universe is. There is nothing between the stars. If you expand your horizons infinitely, you wouldn't be wrong to say there is nothing in outer space. When I think of myself floating alone at a point in space like that, I can't help but think of how confusing and lonely it would be.

For this reason, the thought of outer space makes my heart sink. The universe erases all existence. From a cosmic perspective, the existence of me disappears. If so, it would be like I don't exist, or it doesn't matter that I don't exist. Then why am I living here fretting and complicating? Am I living in an illusion or reality?

To what extent are humans human?

Take my eyes off the universe and look at the human world. What are humans doing? They are observing, analyzing, and understanding the universe. In fact, I know so much about the universe because so many humans have taken the time and effort to figure it out.

Newton described the visible physical world with classical

mechanics, Einstein brought the cosmic view of the physical world (too big to see) into view with relativity, and quantum mechanics, starting with Max Born, allowed us to imagine the microscopic view of the physical world (too small to see). Recently, superstring theory has been working hard to bridge the gap between relativity and quantum mechanics.

I feel a sense of wonder whenever I imagine outer space, but I often feel the same when I think about the world humans are shaping. Whether it's the story of Voyager 1 and 2, which left Earth 46 years ago and are now traveling outside our solar system, or the more recent story of a vending machine-sized spacecraft DART that took ten months to fly on its intended path to the 160-meter-diameter asteroid Dimorphos, 10,800,000 kilometers away, and succeeded in hitting its intended spot and changing its trajectory, how can I listen to the incredible stories of human persistence against all odds without feeling a sense of wonder?

Whether wandering around a megastructure the size of Coex, walking through an apartment building's underground parking garage, driving a car, or sitting in an airplane seat, I cannot but admire their perfection. It is because I think that every artificial structure, such as a complex spatial structure or a single pipe, wire, or even fire extinguisher location, results from clear goals, careful planning, and diligent execution.

What is the power that makes us silently carry out the difficult process until we create the image we have drawn in our heads into reality? I call it willpower. Everything humans have created and discovered is a product of willpower, so the life I live and create daily is also a product of my willpower. From a cosmic point of view, I do not exist, and my living itself becomes vain. But on the other hand, isn't it worth living enough from a human point of view considering the meaning of willpower like this? If the universe is amazing, there is no reason why my living shouldn't be amazing too. Perhaps that's why the ancients compared humans to microcosms.

The story of "yellow-bellied goose bug"

There is a bug named the "yellow-bellied goose bug" because of its yellow abdomen and goose-like overall appearance. Its official name is Cycnotrachelodes cyanopterus. It's often referred to as the architect of the grass because when it's time to lay eggs, the way it rolls up leaves to make its nest is reminiscent of a skillful architect.

I've watched in fascination as a yellow-bellied goose bug builds its nest in a TV documentary. It starts by choosing a leaf of the right size, then using its tiny jaws to chew off a bite from the edge of the leaf, making an extended J-shaped cut. It then bites off one end of the cut, pulls it in with its mouth, grasps it with its six slender legs, and rolls it up while pressing it firmly with its belly.

It can take up to three hours for a yellow-bellied goose bug to complete a nest in this way. Watching them do it, I can't help but be struck by how severe and sincere their attitude is about each step of the process and how tearfully beautiful it is. It is also a reverent scene of the willpower of a single creature. There is no room for distractions. Even though the yellow-bellied goose bug is just an insect, its piety is not lacking in comparison to the piety of the universe.

After watching the yellow-bellied goose bug build its nest, I sometimes think of myself as a yellow-bellied goose bug. Am I living my life with the same sincerity as the yellow-bellied goose bug, unabashedly giving my life its own meaning, even from the cosmic point of view?

If I can look above my head and imagine the universe beyond, and if I can draw my gaze in close and observe the yellow-bellied goose bug still, and if I can feel the beauty of life on these two ends of my gaze, I will be able to balance the illusion and reality that human life inevitably contains. Suppose I repeat this exercise from time to time. In that case, I will gradually develop a sense of balance within myself and be able to accept the fluctuations of emotions that occur in my life as they are.

== KEY POINTS ==

Occasionally, look overhead and imagine the universe beyond, and occasionally, draw your gaze closer and observe the yel-low-bellied goose bug still.

"To live is to take good care of your body"

- 4 tips to feel better right now

In my 20 years as a publishing editor, I've planned, edited, and directed more than 300 kinds of books. They range from psychology, self-help, religion, and business. All of these books teach a "how-to" on a specific topic. Each author generously passes on the know-how they've studied, learned, and practiced. If you follow them diligently enough, you might have results.

An editor is a happy job. I get to learn a lot from authors while editing their books. Especially when it comes to books that deal with the mind and emotions, my mind and emotions heal as I work.

There are many ways to control your emotions, but they all aim the same. That is, How do I find peace of mind? It's "how to find peace of mind." In my experience, the following four ways are sufficient. I'm sure that if you properly practice just one of these four things when you feel your emotions simmer, you'll find stability immediately.

The first is to sleep well.

While we sleep, our brains organize. It keeps what it needs and deletes what it doesn't, so when we wake up, our minds are refreshed. It's because the thoughts in our heads are simplified. The things you worried about just a few minutes ago seem silly.

The second is to eat well.

When we feed our body, we feel energized. If we eat a bowl of hot rice soup when we're shivering on a cold day, mysteriously, the cold disappears immediately. I even feel my car energized when I fill it with gas and drive out of the gas station. I step on the gas pedal, and my car runs forward immediately. Whether it's a car or a person, eating delicious food gives it energy; when it gets energy, it feels better.

The third is to move the body.

Eating food gives us energy, which gives us strength, but exercise paradoxically uses up that energy, which gives us strength. When we burn energy, our body temperature goes up, and when our body temperature goes up, we feel better. It's often said that the energy rises. When my energy rises, I can feel my small world expanding a bit, even if not a lot.

The fourth is meditation.

Whereas sleeping, eating, and moving well is about purifying the body to calm the mind, meditation is about working directly with the mind. The key to meditation is to reach a trance in which all thoughts, even the ego, have disappeared. How you bring yourself into a trance differs for everyone, but I take long walks. For the first hour or so, my mind wanders to the tasks at hand. For the second hour, my thoughts turn inward, and I become solitary. By three hours or more, I've reached a point where my thoughts are gone, so after a long walk, I feel like I awake after a deep sleep.

-*-*-*-*-*-

Professor Do-ol Kim Yong-ok says that "human beings live with their bodies." Therefore, he emphasizes, "What is more important than the liberation of the Buddha or the heaven of Jesus is to keep a body well." It means that any excellent task, such as stabilizing a family, ruling a country, or getting the world, starts with taking care of one's own body.

Sometimes, whenever I listen to Do-ol's saying, I slap my

knees and feel like I get hit in the back of my head. For example, it is exactly what he says like this: "Human beings live with their bodies." He's truly a great scholar when it comes to summarizing the seemingly complex and difficult meaning of "living" in such a simple way.

If everything in life starts with my body, then what I need to do right now becomes clear. It's about sleeping, eating, moving well, and quieting my mind. These are the easy ways to make me feel better right now, but furthermore, they are the starting points that fundamentally change my life.

If you're feeling lost or don't know what to do, you first need to take care of yourself: sleep well, eat well, move well, and calm your mind. Only then can you take control of your emotions and be proactive about taking control of your life.

More Books
for your good life from METASEQUO

The Secret of Harvard Writing
: How to write whatever you want

with only 4 sentences!

by Suki Song

Daughters Grow up Feeding on Mother's Emotions
: Self-Recovery Guide to Heal the Love-Hate

Relationship between Mothers and Daughters

by Woo-ran Park

My Sensitive Child
: Temperament-Based Parenting Tips

from a Child Psychiatrist

by Chi-hyun Choi

Only Changed the Way of Speaking
: 48 Psychological Conversation Skills

with Anyone, Anytime, and Anywhere

by Suhyang Oh